DARKNESS OVER TIBET

By

T. ILLION

Author of
"In Secret Tibet"

DARKNESS OVER TIBET

Copyright 1937
Theodore Illion

First published by
Rider & Co. London.

Printed in the United States of America

This Printing: 1991
ISBN 0-932813-14-3

Published by Adventures Unlimited Press
Box 22, Stelle, Illinois 60919-9989 USA

The Mystic Traveller Series:

•IN SECRET TIBET by Theodore Illion (1937)
•DARKNESS OVER TIBET by Theodore Illion (1938)
•TENTS IN MONGOLIA by Sven Haslund (1934)
•MEN AND GODS IN MONGOLIA by Sven Haslund (1935)
•MYSTERY CITIES by Thomas Gann (1925)
•IN QUEST OF LOST WORLDS by Byron de Prorok (1937)

Adventures Unlimited
Explore the Past...

INTRODUCTION:

The German traveller Theodore Illion was one of the first travellers to penetrate Tibet while it was still sealed off from the outside. Illion, who spoke fluent Tibetan, had to disguise himself as a wandering Tibetan monk in order to escape detection, as it was illegal for any foreigner to be in Tibet.

He began planning his trip in 1932 and left Germany in 1934. After several years of adventures and hairaising narrow escapes with death, he returned to Germany to write *Ratfelhaftes Tibet,* published in Hamburg in 1936. His books were quickly translated into English and published by Rider & Company in London: IN SECRET TIBET (1937) & DARKNESS OVER TIBET (1938).

DARKNESS OVER TIBET, is an extremely rare book. Illion made some chance acquaintances which led to contacts with wise men and black magicians. He then was invited to live and study in an underground city in central Tibet. His subsequent escape and hair-raising journies are classic travel writing of the 1930's. It is believed that Illion's accounts of Tibet were instrumental in persuading the Nazi government of Germany to send yearly expeditions into Tibet. The first volume, IN SECRET TIBET, recounts the first episodes of Illion's fascinating adventures in Central Asia.

T. ILLION

PREFACE

IN my book *In Secret Tibet* I have given an outline of my recent journey to Tibet, showing how, passing through successive contacts with the Tibetan multitude and gangs of brigands, I finally succeeded in visiting Tibetan monasteries in the disguise of a native. After witnessing various marvels, such as the flying lamas and the Tibetan *respas*,* I reached the final stage of the journey in the most inaccessible part of the country where live the genuine Tibetan hermits, who can read people's thoughts and possess the strange power to maintain themselves young almost indefinitely.

My talks with these wise men, which are recorded in my earlier book, reflect a certain degree of understanding of the vital problems of Life and Death, spiritual crimes, Salvation and Eternity, and many of my readers will have wondered how the author arrived at a degree of understanding which made these spiritual contacts possible.

Let me say, then, in this connection, that real understanding in spiritual matters is the result of much bitter fighting, of suffering, spiritual agony and soul passion. Life itself would have no meaning if there was no fighting on *all* planes, if all was smooth and monotonous. Everything fights in nature. Every plant fights to get more sunshine,

---

* People who can sit naked and motionless for several hours during icily cold nights without freezing to death.

v

every animal fights for food ; *the angels themselves fight*. Constant struggle on all planes to which it has access is the birthright of the creature. Woe to him who wants to put himself on a level with the Creator and escape fighting !

I had bitter experiences too. On my travels I have met some of the highest spiritual entities incarnated in the flesh, and not only those working for the Creator but also those working against him.

Even the fires of hell have their mission. They destroy man if he is weak, but if he is strong they purify by burning the dross away.

This book supplements *In Secret Tibet* by showing a different side of the picture, a few Demons of Light and many Demons of the Shadow. It will help the reader to realize that spirituality actually is a very stormy ocean. The currents of life are inter-woven, and Good and Evil, Light and Shadow, are within a hairbreadth from each other.

The existence of an Underground City in Tibet is occasionally hinted at by well-informed people in the forbidden country, although the stories are often extravagant and turn the Underground City, which I succeeded in entering, into a "Mighty Underground Empire inhabited by millions of people".

Tibet becomes somewhat more accessible as the years roll by, and I am confident that eventually other explorers will confirm my description of the Underground City of Tibet.

T. ILLION.

CONTENTS

Gods and Demons guard the main temple of Lhasa

Darkness Over Tibet

CHAPTER I

HUNTED BY TIBETAN BRIGANDS

KE SHU KHA RU, the Tibetan brigand boy who ran
away from his gang to join me in the lone solitudes
of mysterious Tibet and who probably met a horrible
death as a result of this independent attitude, was
a bright young Tibetan whose brother, a stately
robber, had induced the boy to join his own gang
of bandits preying on unprotected travellers in
western Tibet. The boy was grossly "uneducated"
in the Western sense of the word, but nevertheless
was very clever.

My talks with this youthful Tibetan brigand—he
was hardly seventeen years old when we travelled
together—stand out as one of my bright and painful
experiences in Tibet. His remarks on Western
countries, although made in a humorously naïve
and childlike manner, were almost a revelation to
me in many respects. In judging Western civili-
zation, Ke Shu Kha Ru, who had never heard
anything about the West before, had the priceless
advantage of viewing things in an absolutely
unprejudiced manner, like someone from another
planet. When listening to him I felt like a person

who has never left his own house, and therefore does not really know what it is like until he steps out of it and has a good look at it from outside.

Ke Shu Kha Ru was a member of the gang of robbers who attacked me in the early morning in a swampy district and with whom I had the amusing adventure recorded in my earlier book. One of the bandits had made a short cut across the swamp in order to be the first to rob me. He had left his comrades a long way behind him. When the swamp swallowed him up to his chest I saved his life and thus made friends with the whole gang.

While we were having breakfast together and talking about travels and other countries, an exceptionally young member of the gang, I noted, a boy of about sixteen or seventeen, was watching me continually with brilliant eyes.

"How nice it must be not to be afraid," I heard him say admiringly to another brigand. After this remark the boy showed me his tongue again and again, which is a mark of high esteem in Tibet.

A quarter of an hour later the brigands wished me "a slow journey".*

When they all smiled and showed me their tongues in parting, only the boy seemed to turn away.

I walked away in a southerly direction. The bandits moved northward. When I turned round I saw that he appeared to be lagging behind.

* The Tibetans use the term "slow journey" when really wishing a safe or happy journey, the very word "slow" having an auspicious meaning in the eyes of the Tibetans. The term "fast" has a rather unpleasant significance in Tibet. It is often associated with speed, cunning, and violence.

The brigands shouted his name twice and the boy followed them, to all appearance rather reluctantly.

For many hours I kept up a brisk pace. It was not until the wind began to blow in the afternoon that I sat down to take a good rest, having walked about twenty miles since I had parted company with the robbers.

I felt a little tired and sleepy. It was the fourth week spent at an altitude of 15,000 feet while living on inadequate food and walking daily enormous distances in the thin mountain air.

The wind had just begun to whirl up little clouds of fine sand which somewhat obscured the vision in the mildly undulating landscape bordered by high mountains in the distance, when a tiny little black spot appeared amidst the whirling sand. At first I thought it was an animal, but after a few minutes the moving figure grew larger and I saw that it walked upright. It was a human being, walking straight towards the place where I was seated.

The chances of meeting another human being in the uninhabited expanses of northern Tibet are not greater than the prospect of winning a good-sized prize in a lottery. I could hardly believe my eyes.

When the solitary wanderer was within a distance of a few yards he stopped and stared at me spellbound. I recognized him. It was the Tibetan brigand boy who had watched me earlier in the day.

"*Oh gyagg, oh gyagg*,"* said Ke Shu Kha Ru.

It was my turn to be greatly astonished at meeting

---

* Polite greeting used in northern Tibet. It really means : "You are making an effort."

the youngster whom I had seen moving in the
opposite direction half a day before.

In all probability this boy had been forced to
take up the robber's profession against his wish.
He had seen a man travelling about quite alone in
the desert who had not been afraid of a gang of
robbers. This may have appealed strongly to the
innate thirst of adventure and horror of mediocrity
which are so common in boys of his age. For boys
seem to be the same all over the world. Most of
them are full of enthusiasm until they lose their
high spirits by the bad example set by other people
and the hard necessities of life. In fighting the
depressing influence of their surroundings for years
and years most people succeed only outwardly.
Their better selves are gradually twisted round and
crippled in the struggle which boys of that age still
have to face.

After leaving his comrades the Tibetan boy, as
he told me later, had felt lonely and therefore
decided to join me by following my footprints as
fast as he could.

Ke Shu Kha Ru looked at me inquiringly. I was
in deep thought, weighing the situation.

Like most other things in life, the sudden appearance of the young Tibetan seemed to be a very
mixed blessing.

If the boy was not as tough as wire he would be
a dreadful hindrance by his inability to stand the
physical strain of my rapid movements. Furthermore, sooner or later he would find out that I was
a white person.

On the other hand, the boy could be of some use.

If he was reliable and could stand the strain of heavy marches while living on small amounts of uncooked food, I could make him talk to the people and hold myself entirely in the background, thus further diminishing the chances of detection.

Ke Shu Kha Ru was strong and well built. His clothes were in good shape. He had brought along sufficient food for several days as well as a small bag filled with dry dung. He wore high leather shoes of excellent quality. The gang had obviously picked out the very cream of the belongings of their victims for personal use. He was fairly clean and the expression of his eyes and features denoted exceptional energy and intelligence.

I decided to take a chance with him. In any case it was impossible to chase him out into the desert.

The boy got ready to cook a meal. He opened the bag containing dried dung and his cooking utensils for making tea. He was greatly surprised and almost annoyed when I forbade him to kindle a fire, adding that as long as he travelled in my company I should never allow him to do so, neither for warming himself nor for cooking. After some reflection Ke Shu Kha Ru seemed to guess the reason of this precaution, which greatly increases the safety of unprotected travellers, and with an energetic movement he threw away his bag filled with dung.

It was very strange to have a companion after so many weeks of solitary travelling. The brigand boy unpacked his belongings. Everything was almost new and fairly clean. The choice of the various items indicated much good taste and a practical and matter-of-fact attitude of the owner. I thought that if I took the boy along to the West after completing my journey in Tibet he would adapt himself to Western conditions much faster than any other Tibetan I had met so far.

Early in the morning he began to take off his clothes in order to "wash" in the Tibetan manner by rubbing his body with a good-sized pat of butter. He then came to me with another piece of butter and was greatly surprised when he saw that I refused to "wash". He probably thought I was a very unclean person.

While Ke Shu Kha Ru mused about the strange ways of his newly found companion I thought of the best possible method of telling the boy that I was a white person. Unless I told him myself, he would sooner or later find it out himself. The withholding of such a secret from a clever companion sharing every moment of one's existence in the uninhabited wastes of Central Asia required much ingenuity and great discomfort, including the necessity of my abstaining from washing!

After having partaken of an uncooked meal, when we were on our way again I told the boy that I was half a day late and contemplated walking all day from morning till night. He did not seem to mind this.

We did a good deal of talking.

"Why are you not afraid?" asked the boy. "I watched you there on the dry island in the swamp. When your enemy approached threateningly you stood there, quietly watching him."

"One does not make things better by being

HUNTED BY TIBETAN BRIGANDS 15

afraid, Ke Shu Kha Ru," I replied. "We must take things in life as they come. It is stupid to defy dangers. But when dangers do come our way we should face them coolly."

"I greatly admired you there," said the boy, "but when the bandit was dragged down by the swamp and you threw the rope out to save his life, I was greatly surprised."

"I saved him," I answered, "assuming that he had a soul."

"What is that?"

"The thing that is best in us. Our real self. People who have a soul react to kindness. If you save an aggressor's life and he happens to have a soul, he is disarmed. His soul will prevent him from attacking his rescuer."

"Will all people feel disarmed by boundless kindness and love?"

"No, Ke Shu Kha Ru," I answered sadly, "not everybody. Only people who have a soul. But many people have a soul."

"Tell me," said the Tibetan brigand, "suppose the man whose life you saved by pulling him out of the swamp had attacked you immediately afterwards. What would you have done then?"

"I should have seen that he had no soul and should have pushed him back into the murderous swamp immediately."

"Do you think that I have a soul?" asked the boy.

I looked into his eyes. "Yes, Ke Shu Kha Ru," I answered, "you have."

"Can man lose his soul?"

"Yes, I think so, but not all at once.   It is a slow and dreadful process."

"How can he lose it ?"

"By sinning against his soul."

"How ?"

"By brutalizing his soul; by using God for selfish purposes."

"What is God ?"

Dear me, now I had landed in a theological discussion with a Tibetan brigand.   My knowledge of colloquial Tibetan was no longer up to the occasion.   Anyhow, I had to go on with it.

"God is the one who made you," I said.

"*Kho byas pa ma yin*,"* remarked Ke Shu Kha Ru.   "My father made me."

"*Kyod-di lus byas pa yin*,"† I said, "but God made your soul.   He is the Father of your soul."

"Also of yours ?"

"Yes, also of mine."

"So we are brothers ?"

"Yes, we are.   The same Father made our souls."

His eyes sparkled.   "I am glad you are my brother."

After a slight pause he asked :

"And the people who have no soul . . . who is *their* father ?"

"They were children of our Father," I answered sadly, "but the great black God‡ possesses their souls."

"Has he taken it ?"

"Yes—or rather, they have given it to him."

---

* "He did not make me."   † "He made your body."
‡ *Lha-gnag-chenpo.*

"Could *Lha-gnag-chenpo* take our souls too?"

"No, he cannot, unless we give them to him voluntarily."

"But tell me who has more power: the Father who made our souls, or the great black God?"

"Our Father," I replied, "is more powerful."

"Why does he not crush the great black God?"

"The great black God hates the Father," I said, "but in his blind *dang** he really guards the Father's house. If someone wants to be like the Father, if a creature wants to be like the Creator, the great black God seizes his soul."

"I no longer understand this," said the young brigand.

I changed the topic. Drops of perspiration were standing on my forehead. So great had been the effort to discuss such problems in broken Tibetan.

I walked faster and faster. The boy smiled and walked faster still to show me that he was not tired at all and meant to be a first-class companion full of stamina.

"Are you afraid of death?" he asked after a little while.

His mind was obviously running on deep problems. Practical as he was, he was nevertheless under the spell of the Tibetan conception of things. Abstruse and spiritual considerations play a much more important part in the lives of the Tibetans than the matter-of-fact problems which occupy the minds of white people in the first place.

"No, I am not afraid of death," I answered. "If

---

* Hatred.

I die, my soul will not be separated from the Father. Real death is the death of the soul. The death of the body is not so dreadful, although it is painful for those who love us."

"Have you ever loved anybody ?"

"Yes. And when I love, I love very intensely, with my whole being and indescribable soul-passion."

"Is not life wonderful ?"

"It is, although it gives suffering too."

"Suffering only increases the pleasures of subsequent enjoyment," observed Ke Shu Kha Ru with a merry laugh.

Can one imagine a Western boy making such a remark ?

I again increased the speed. We now walked at something like four miles an hour in the thin mountain air. The boy did not show the slightest sign of fatigue. I was determined not to propose a rest until he would ask for it himself. But the distance covered grew longer and longer.

"Do you like someone ?" he asked suddenly.

"Yes," I said.

"Whom ?"

"Everybody who has a soul."

"No one in particular ?"

"Not at present."

"No friends ?"

"Hundreds and thousands," I answered, "but yet I am very lonely."

"I like you," he said.

"Why ?"

"Because you are a big boy. You are so simple

and yet clever, and your goodness is strength and not weakness. I know it . . . you are older, but still a boy like me. . . . Tell me, how shall I call you?"

"*Bod-laa min ba ma yin*,"* I said after some hesitation.

"No name in Tibet. . . . Tell me also, why do you speak Tibetan so badly? With the brigands you talked so little. Then I hardly noticed it. But now that you speak at great length I cannot help noticing it. I really don't know what to think of you."

He looked at me fully with his big clever eyes.

"Have you already heard something about white people, Ke Shu Kha Ru?" I asked him.

"Yes. . . . They must be terrible monsters."

"Really?"

"Certainly. People without hearts. Ugly—disgusting—bad—cruel—terrible—inhuman. . . ."

"All of them?"

"Yes, *all* of them, without a single exception!"

"Who told you this, Ke Shu Kha Ru?"

"The bandits, and also my family. We have it from the priests."

"Would you recognize a white person here in Tibet?"

"I bet I would. Even if he was in the cleverest disguise, he would betray himself by his horrible smell. It is a well-known fact that white people stink so terribly that *Bod-pas*† would be taken ill when getting within half a kosatsa [hearing distance] from them."

"Are you so certain that this is true?"

---

* "I have no name in Tibet."   † Tibetans.

"But, of course. We know it from people of whom we believe everything."

"Now listen, Ke Shu Kha Ru. What would you do if you caught a white person here in Tibet ?"

I watched his face with considerable suspense.

"I do not know," he replied hesitatingly, "I really never thought of it." After a slight pause he added : "Most Tibetans would arrest him at once and hand the white monster over to the lamas."

"What would the lamas do with him ?"

"I have heard that they would push him down into a deep shaft. There he would fall on a mass of human corpses and slowly die from hunger and thirst."

"If I happened to be a white person, would it be my fault ?" I asked suddenly, opening my blue eyes fully and undoing the leather strap under my chin, laying bare my white chest.

The Tibetan boy recoiled as if he had been dealt a deadly blow and almost gasped. Cold drops of perspiration appeared on his forehead.

"What, you—*you*, you are a white man ?" he stammered.

"Is it my fault, Ke Shu Kha Ru ?" I observed quietly.

He sat down, terror-stricken.

"But then I was told lies," he said after a little while. "You are not a monster at all . . . but you, just *you*, are a white person. . . . How dreadful !"

"Will you give me away to the priests ?"

He looked at me fully. For the first time I saw tears in his eyes.

"No, I shall not."

"Can I be sure of it ?"

"Absolutely."

"That is nice of you, Ke Shu Kha Ru."

"If others found you out in Tibet and the priests would throw you down into the shaft . . ."

"Well ?"

"Oh, nothing, nothing."

I gave him a little time to get over the shock he had received, and then asked with a faint smile :

"Don't you run away from me now, Ke Shu Kha Ru, now that you know that I am an evil-smelling monster, ugly, disgusting, bad, cruel, terrible, inhuman. . . ."

"No," he said quietly, "the lamas and brigands have told lies, and then, is it your fault that you were born in the West ?"

"No," I said, "I was much too young at that time to choose a *skye-sa*." *

We both had a good laugh. A very critical moment of my travels in Tibet had passed.

How broad-minded Ke Shu Kha Ru must have been to dismiss in a moment all the prejudices gradually hammered into his head during the course of many years ! . . . Is it not a fact that there is something in certain people which lifts them greatly above the limitations of heredity and environment ?

The cloud had passed and we took a well-earned rest, munching raw barley-meal mixed with a little rancid butter.

When both of us stopped munching, and neither of us moved or talked, I became aware of

------

* Birthplace.

the silence of death hanging over the desert. It was ghastly in its monotony. Only people living in western Tibet or Ladakh occasionally walk out alone into the desert. The inhabitants of eastern Tibet never do so. They say that the silence and the demons would kill them.

In the dead silence, which is so complete that one's ears begin to buzz, the sound of a human voice sounds like sweet music. Small wonder that people who live alone for months in such environs get into the habit of talking aloud to themselves.

A quarter of an hour later we were on our way again. The young Tibetan seemed very keen on learning something about "the country where people have bleached faces".

"How far is it from here to *Pee-lin-pa* ?"*

"Immeasurably far," I answered.

"Where is it ?"

I pointed westward.

"And what lies here ?" he asked, pointing southward.

"*Gyadkar*,"† I answered.

"And there ?"—he pointed eastward.

"*Gyadnag*,"‡ I said.

"How many days' ride is it from here to *Pee-lin-pa* ?"

"Many months. But white people travel much faster than Tibetans do. Once a man has left *Tö-bod*§ he travels tremendously fast."

"How ?"

---

* The country of the white people.
† *Gyadkar*—the white expansion (India).
‡ *Gyadnag*—the black expansion (China).
§ High Tibet.

I thought of motor-cars and railways. There are no Tibetan words to describe them.

"White people travel in rectangular frames rolling on coins which are four times the size of your head."

"How extraordinary. Tell me, are *gyags** put to these frames ?"

"No, there are no yaks in the country of the white people."

"What sort of animals are used for pulling the frames ?"

"There are no animals at all. The frames go all by themselves."

"Do white people use ghosts then, to pull their frames ?"

"No. Ghosts do not serve white people."

"Surely something must pull those frames. What is it ?"

"*Me*† does it. . . . Just as you eat your barley-meal and animals eat *tsa*‡ to keep going, the frames used by white people eat fire."

"Fire ! Does it not burn their mouths ?"

"No. They have no mouths at all. Only people and animals have *kha-nam*.§ The frames have none."

"How can they eat then ?"

I scratched my head. Surely, it was difficult to describe technical details to Ke Shu Kha Ru. How could I quickly wriggle out of this tight corner so that the boy should not think I had contradicted myself ? I thought it over.

"You just said they eat," remarked the Tibetan

---

* Yaks.
‡ Grass.
† Fire.
§ Mouths.

emphatically, "and now you say they have no mouths ! Please explain."

I once more imagined a motor-car. What a fix I was in !

I had a bright idea. "Look here," I said, "have you ever pulled a shrub out of the earth ?"

"Yes," he said.

"What did you see in the ground then ?"

"Little wooden pipes by which the plant feeds itself."

"Well," I said, "the fire-eating frames get their food through metal pipes."

"Out of the ground ?"

Decidedly, I had to give up giving technical details. I tried to explain things by means of a sketch rapidly drawn on a piece of paper, but in spite of his remarkable intelligence Ke Shu Kha Ru could not make head or tail of it. It was probably the first time in his life that he had ever seen a drawing.

"How difficult it is to understand *Pee-lin-pa*," he said with a sigh. "Never mind all these details. I gather from what you say that the frames eat fire. Anyhow, they must have excellent digestions and no doubt a good deal of smoke comes out from them from behind."

"Not precisely from behind, but there is some *dud-pa*,* anyhow."

"Tell me," he went on, "do these fire-eating frames move fast ?"

"Often fifteen times faster than the fastest yaks can go."

Tibetan yaks usually move along placidly at the

---

* Smoke.

rate of less than two miles an hour, so there was no exaggeration in saying that modern means of transport move fifteen times faster.

"How extraordinary," observed Ke Shu Kha Ru. "Fire-eating frames moving fifteen times faster than yaks . . . Tell me, *why* do white people want to travel fifteen times faster than we do ? Why ?"

"White people want to travel faster," I said after some hesitation, "because they want to be happy. The faster they travel and the higher houses they build, the more they think they will be happy."

"And *are* white people happier than we are ?" the clever boy went on asking with rather embarrassing consistency.

"No," I said, feeling rather ashamed. "They are not happier than the Tibetans."

"This is very strange," Ke Shu Kha Ru went on. "White people use fire-eating frames to be happy, they build *kanpa-mthon-po*,* as you say, in order to be happy, and yet you say they are not happier than we, who have no fire-devouring frames and no high houses. . . . Why ?"

There was a long pause.

"Why ?" he asked again. "Tell me why."

"Listen, Ke Shu Kha Ru," I answered. "White people seem to be afflicted with a strange *nad*.† They invent more and more ; they make life more and more comfortable, but while they are doing all this they complicate their lives more and more and create additional needs, so in the end they are not better off than in the beginning."

A hailstorm had come on rather suddenly. They

---

* Very high houses.   † Disease.

are very frequent in Tibet in the summer. Enormous hailstones were coming down and I could feel their impact through my thick Tibetan clothes. When we found that some of the hailstones were the size of a walnut we lay flat on the ground and covered ourselves up with our belongings, waiting patiently until the hailstorm was over.

It lasted only ten minutes, leaving the ground covered with a layer of ice several inches thick.

Then the sun came out, the air became as clear as crystal, once more illustrating the fact that Tibet is a country of the greatest contrasts climatically. We had shivered with cold two minutes before and now the heat was almost tropical. Huge masses of ice disappeared rapidly in the hot sunshine and small torrents appeared everywhere. We knew that the ground would be fairly dry very soon and remained seated for some time.

Our talk about Western countries had greatly excited Ke Shu Kha Ru's interest and imagination, and as soon as the hailstorm had passed he reverted to the same topic.

"You said that white people are in the habit of complicating life and creating additional needs," he observed. "I am very curious to know *what* they are doing to complicate life."

I thought of the difficulty I had experienced a short while ago when trying to give him a description of a motor-car. To convey to him an idea of Western complications was no small job. Furthermore, the Tibetan language is not at all suitable for giving any descriptions of a technical nature.

When used for describing material things Tibetan is very primitive and leaves but little margin for expressing details.

Only in describing spiritual and immaterial things Tibetan permits of expressing an enormously wide range of shades of meaning. I heard at least six different terms in Tibetan to translate the English word "hermit".* For such ideas as "meditation" or "spirituality" there is a voluminous vocabulary. In spiritual matters many Tibetan words require a whole sentence to convey their meaning in English.† But it is just the opposite where material things are concerned. Then, in many instances, one English word may require several dozen Tibetan words to convey even an approximate idea of its meaning.

It was no use trying to describe complicated Western machinery and conveniences to the young Tibetan. So I started with complications of the simpler variety and mentioned smoking in the first place. Even then it was difficult enough. As smoking is unknown in most parts of Tibet there is no Tibetan word for it.

I said, then, "White people often adopt the habit of putting small chimneys into their mouths and blowing *dud-pa* out of their noses."

Ke Shu Kha Ru laughed heartily and then asked :

---

* *Gsans-pa, gom-tshen, bdag-shrun, bsam-gtan-pa, nallior-pa,* and *res-pa !* Perhaps the reader will try to learn these six terms by heart to get an idea of how difficult it is to learn Tibetan.

† For instance, the Tibetan word *dondenpai-denpa* means " the sort of self-consciousness which gives one an erroneous conception of the real value of things".

"But how can they keep the chimney in their mouths?"

"It is a *small* chimney, Ke Shu Kha Ru," I answered; "it is not difficult to keep it in the mouth at all."

"Nevertheless, I am sure, small as it is, it does fall out continually," he said.

"Why?" I asked, astonished.

"Well, if someone puts a small chimney into his *kha** and blows smoke out of his nose he must be so shaken with laughter that the chimney drops from his mouth."

"No, Ke Shu Kha Ru," I observed, "white people never laugh when putting chimneys into their mouths."

Ke Shu Kha Ru absolutely refused to believe me. Whatever I put forward to convince him of the contrary he repeated again and again:

"*Dsun ba yin, dsun ba yin.*"†

"Look here, boy," I said, after a good deal of unsuccessful persuasion, "once people get used to strange things they cease to laugh about them. You have many strange things here in Tibet about which you never laugh. You have had them for centuries, but you fail to see their comical side because they have lasted so long that you have got used to them. Nearly all people live and think habitually."

We then talked about Tibet for many hours. The boy was very clever and an excellent observer. The few dozen remarks he made about his countrymen showed deep understanding and threw very

---

* Mouth.   † "It can't be true."

much light on Tibetan conditions and the mentality of the Tibetans.

Ke Shu Kha Ru placed great confidence in me and treated me like a friend whom he might have known ten years. Suddenly he asked :

"Tell me, are white boys very different from me ?"

"No," I answered, "not very. Boys are very much the same all over the world. Most of them are full of enthusiasm and sincerity."

"And grown-up people ?"

"In many cases, both their enthusiasm and sincerity diminish as the years roll by," I said sadly.

"Are grown-up people very different in various countries ?"

"Yes, very."

"Why ?"

I tried to convey to him that lack of enthusiasm and sincerity finds expression in many different ways, which differ widely, whereas sincerity and simplicity leave no room for diversity, and that was why boys were so alike all over the world ; but my knowledge of Tibetan was too limited to make the boy understand exactly what I meant.

"I should like to meet white boys," said Ke Shu Kha Ru suddenly.

"If you are very useful to me during my travels here in Tibet," I said, "I may take you back with me to *Pee-lin-pa.*"

His enthusiasm knew no bounds.

"Is the language of the *Pee-lins** very difficult ?"

"No," I replied, "it is very easy." I thought of

---

* White people.

how dreadfully difficult it had been for me to learn Tibetan.

"By the way," I said, "there are many *Pee-lin* languages, but at least one of them, English, is known all over *Pee-lin-pa*."

"What does 'one' mean in the most useful language of the *Pee-lins*?"

"One," I replied.

"Vann," he repeated ("Vann" means "power" in Tibetan). "Vann, Vann, Vann. . . . This is very simple. I shall not forget it."

In less than an hour the clever boy had learned two dozen English words. The word "go" he learned by remembering the Tibetan word *mgo* or *go* (head), the word "come" by *skom* or *kom* (thirst), etc.

So painstaking was he in his effort, and put me to so much work, that we both felt tired after an hour or so. While we talked we had, of course, been walking all the time in the thin mountain air at a speed of about four miles an hour.

He reverted to the problem of white boys. This topic seemed to be of special appeal to him.

"Tell me," he asked, "if a white boy came to Tibet, what would he laugh at?"

"Well, perhaps at your fear of ghosts."

We halted to take some food.

"Everybody here seems to be afraid of ghosts," he observed, after we had started munching un- cooked barley-meal, which he swallowed very bravely. "Even the bandits, otherwise very courageous fellows, are afraid of them. They people even the dunghills with evil spirits. My little brother was murdered by them."

"*Ga-zug ?*"* I asked.

"Evil spirits knocked during the night at the door of the house of my parents. The poor little boy called *nandu kyod*† while he was still only half-awake. Thus the demons got hold of him. He caught fever and died some time afterwards."

As he thought of his little brother his eyes revealed great soul-passion and an immense capacity for suffering. He seemed to be quite different from many other Tibetans who seemed to me to be incapable of such deep feelings.

"Are *you* never annoyed by evil spirits ?" he asked after a slight pause.

"No," I answered.

"Why ?"

"Probably because I am not afraid of them."

Suddenly the young Tibetan seized my arm and pointed northward, whence we had just come. At a distance of a little over a mile a group of people was moving towards us.

"*Gyog-pas !*"‡ he cried.

We finished our meal and marched on southward. The bandits were not mounted, and still a long way behind us. So I hoped we might be able to make our escape by marching on as fast as possible.

However, the faster we went the faster we were followed by the bandits. It was a most unusual experience to be hunted by brigands in uninhabited territories. What on earth could induce a gang of robbers to move across this barren part of Tibet where not even nomads lived ?

The bandits patiently followed our footprints,

* "How ?"   † Come in.   ‡ "Robbers !"

keeping up a brisk pace, and at nightfall, in spite of all our efforts, our lead had hardly increased to one mile and a half.

If the brigands intended to follow us during the night they would have to light torches to see our footprints.   As long as no light was visible at a distance we were safe until daybreak, but, tired as we were, the boy and I had to keep a strenuous look-out alternately all night.

It certainly was a painful necessity to sacrifice half a night's rest after walking thirty to thirty-five miles the previous day.

Soon before sunrise we were on our way again. A quarter of an hour later we again saw the robbers at a distance.   There was no vegetation in the district. Footprints were very easy to follow, and the undulating character of the landscape permitted to see people approaching at a considerable distance. We marched as fast as we could, but the faster we walked the more the bandits increased their speed. By about noon our advance had increased to something like two miles and from time to time the gang entirely disappeared from vision.   The time had come for trying to mislead the robbers.

When we reached a small salt-water lake in a depression we both entered the lake and walked on for some time parallel to the shore.   Then we took a good jump, touching the ground well beyond the water-line and marched off at top speed at right angles to our previous direction. When we reached a mass of debris we went into hiding behind it to take some rest.

About half an hour later the brigands arrived at

the lake. They saw at once that we had entered it and began to walk round it to find the place where we had left the lake. From the place where we were in hiding we could see them very clearly, as the air was as clear as crystal.

To his terror, Ke Shu Kha Ru recognized the robbers. They were his own gang, from whom he had fled! He recognized his brother, who came in rank next to the leader. Obviously the robbers had decided to fetch back their colleague and that was why we were hunted in entirely uninhabited territories!

The situation was far from pleasant. Other brigands who would have no special reason to overtake us apart from their desire to rob us might have given up the pursuit once they had lost our track; but in this case it was to be expected that the bandits would not leave a stone unturned to get hold of us.

Ke Shu Kha Ru absolutely refused to go back to them voluntarily. Moreover, now that he knew that I was a white person he realized that further contacts with the gang might lead to very serious trouble as far as I was concerned.

The bandits closely followed the water-line and walked past the place where we had jumped out of the lake. It would take them nearly an hour to walk round the lake before they realized that they had been baffled and began to walk round the salt lake in a wider circle.

Ke Shu Kha Ru, who seemed to be thoroughly fed up with his brigand's job, exulted. He was determined to get away from the gang as much as I was myself. A quarter of an hour later the bandits were far enough to make it possible for us to leave the place where we were in hiding. We crawled up to the next ridge, which was a few hundred yards distant, and the earthen colour of my tent thrown over us stood us in very good stead.

As soon as we were beyond the ridge we marched off eastward as fast as we could, putting in a few hundred yards' run from time to time. We stopped for short periods only to eat, and when night had fallen we kept up a watch alternately.

During the second half of the night the boy awakened me. A faint glow of fire was visible in the distance.

The bandits had probably realized that we were much too resourceful and energetic fellows to be caught at all unless they took up pursuit by day and by night. Having walked round the lake a first time they had realized that we had been tricky enough to make them walk four miles in vain, thus gaining a tremendous advantage. They had begun to walk round the lake a second time in a much wider circle until they had found our new track, and when our footsteps showed them that we had walked and run alternately they understood that they would never get hold of such tough customers unless they decided to sacrifice a night's rest to continue the pursuit.

We marched on in the darkness, the stars showing the direction. Ke Shu Kha Ru, tired as he was, seemed to view the whole affair in a sporting manner and stood the test very bravely. In addition to strong feelings and bright intelligence, he seemed to have a powerful will.

He began to talk. I brought home to him that we were in for a desperate fight and could not afford to lose the slightest amount of physical strength, all our lung capacity being necessary for getting along as fast as we could.

As soon as we reached a place suitable for wiping out our footprints and misleading our pursuers, we suddenly changed our direction and moved off southward.

Half an hour later the sun rose.

The boy's feet began to blister a little. Brave as he was, the depressing effect of exhaustion made itself felt. Living mostly on uncooked barley-meal, walking and running forty-five miles in a day and having only half a night's rest can affect even a strong and healthy man.

"*Ga-ʒug tsho-tshe?*"* he asked again and again. After a while he added sadly :

"You must not be taken prisoner by the lamas. My brother is a *myi-bʒan-po*,† but if we are caught and he finds out that you are a white person, the worst may happen and he may hand you over to the priests."

After a short rest we marched on non-stop for about ten hours. The boy's feet blistered more and more, but he absolutely refused to stop. When I offered to take him on my back he bit his lips and said firmly :

"*Me, me, me.*"‡

Then I approached him and got hold of him to put him on my back by sheer force, as I had seen a few drops of blood colouring his footprints ; but he

---

* "What can we do ?"   † A good man.   ‡ "No, no, no."

resisted vigorously, and I finally had to give up trying to get hold of him.

Our situation had become quite desperate. On reaching the top of a particularly high ridge we could see the brigands, who had made up a considerable part of the distance separating us, and again followed us at a distance of about two and a half miles. I must explain in this connection that in the desolate expanses of northern and central Tibet, which are devoid of vegetation and where the air is as clear as crystal, people approaching at a distance are visible many miles away, if they do not happen to be hidden by a ridge.

It was obvious that we should be caught the subsequent night if the robbers decided to march on by the light of a torch, which was very probable. Moreover, even if we could avoid them by an almost miraculous turn of good luck, our food supply was running out rapidly and the cutting down of food rations would have to be started in a day or two.

Then Nature herself came to our assistance.

Just when we marched through a depression late in the afternoon there suddenly came a rumble as if a hundred railway trains passed underground in the immediate vicinity. Big boulders and debris rolled down from all sides. It was the first of a series of earthquakes I had to face in Tibet during the next few days. It lasted several minutes and was so violent that it was difficult to keep one's feet.

Ke Shu Kha Ru calmly dodged the stones and seemed to be quite used to this sort of thing, but more and more blood appeared in his footprints.

It was probable that the earthquake had affected a very extensive area, wiping out our footprints radically. Most probably the gang would have lost our track.

Since we were both tired to death we put up the tent as quickly as possible and soon fell asleep.

When I awoke it must have been about noon the subsequent day. It was raining very fast. I looked round. Ke Shu Kha Ru had disappeared.

I looked out. No one was within sight. I shouted in all directions. No answer! What had happened to the boy?

I walked out into the rain to examine the surroundings. Torrential rain had wiped out all footprints. I had not the slightest clue pointing to his whereabouts. As a portion of his belongings were still in the tent it was impossible to guess whether he had the intention to return when he left it or not.

I waited for hours, going out from time to time, shouting his name at the top of my voice. Nothing could be heard except the continual fall of heavy rain.

Evening came, and the boy had not yet returned.

Maybe the poor chap had gone out for a short while during the night, intending to return immediately, and had lost his way and gone out into the desert. This occasionally happens to Tibetans. The Tibetan multitudes believe that under the influence of invisible demons the sense of bearing of men leaving their tents in a desert may be temporarily lost, so that they walk in the wrong direction and cannot find their way back to their tents, to the great joy of the demons watching their victim going to his death in the desert.

If the poor boy had made the dreadful mistake of losing his way he was likely to go to certain death. He had neither the geographical knowledge nor the experience of a man who had crossed alone the various deserts of the world, and would walk about in circles and die miserably of hunger and exposure.

All night I kept a sharp look-out. During the second half of the night the rain stopped, and soon afterwards I kindled a small fire to show him the way in case he had gone astray.

Morning came and Ke Shu Kha Ru had not yet returned.

I knew it was my duty to wait, although every minute of my time was precious. Northern Tibet would be snowbound in a couple of months, making it impossible for me to return if I hesitated too long ; and by far the larger part of the work for which I had undertaken the expedition and faced all the attending hardships and privations was still ahead of me. I also realized that it was impossible for me to stay in disguise in the forbidden country during the whole winter without being found out.

Just now, when after enormous efforts and hardships I finally was within a few hundred miles from the goal of my journey—the mysterious monasteries and hermits—I was in duty bound to stop for some time in order to wait for this poor boy lost in the desolate expanses of Tibet.

All I could do for him was to wait for some days, keeping watch day and night and lighting a small fire during three successive nights to show him the way.

I had not the slightest clue as to where to seek him, and I fully realized that by roaming about in those uninhabited territories I had no greater chance to find him than a man looking for a little pin in a haystack. Moreover, my food supply was now running out very rapidly.

All I could do was to signal my presence during the night. I even sacrificed a small portion of my equipment in order to keep burning the little fire which I kindled every hour during several nights. In the daytime I could do nothing except wait. Had I left the immediate neighbourhood of the tent I should have run the risk that the boy might have found me absent on his return. He could not read, so I could not leave a message.

After three days I started southward, in a semi-starved condition, with infinite sadness in my heart.

Up to this day the fate of Ke Shu Kha Ru remains a mystery. Did he actually lose his way, meeting a slow and terrible death from starvation and exposure? Or did he leave me voluntarily because he felt that his presence was an additional danger to me? Or did the brigands find our track after all and take the boy back without wishing to work harm to me, since I had rescued the life of one of the members of their gang a few days earlier?

Taking all in all, however, the first alternative—unfortunately—remains by far the most probable one.

What thoughts may have crossed the mind of this clever and kind-hearted boy while he wandered about there in the barren solitude, slowly dying from hunger and exposure ?

Is it credible that the splendid unit of bright intelligence, intense feeling, and strong will-power cloaked into a sheath of matter which I met in the physical form of Ke Shu Kha Ru was a mere chance creation of heredity and environment ? Is it probable that when this bud, just about to open into a flower, was cut off by Fate and dropped dying on the ground of the desert, the supreme goal of this soul should have been annihilation ?

Perhaps many years hence some solitary wanderer will come across a heap of bleached bones in the desolate wastes of western Tibet. Is that all that is left of Ke Shu Kha Ru ?

CHAPTER II

DEMONS DESCENDING

A VERY large number of Tibetan monasteries—and perhaps the most mysterious ones—have never been visited by white people. They vary considerably in size, location, and the attitude of the monks to the visitor, who, in most cases, however, is treated like a welcome milch-cow possessed of only a moderate amount of discrimination and resourcefulness and therefore open to be mulcted very thoroughly, regardless of the fact whether he happens to be *tshugpo** or poor.

Some of the monasteries, like Tashi-Gembe, are very small and accommodate not more than perhaps three hundred monks ; others are at least ten times larger. Some of the monasteries, such as the Dsog-tshen monastery, are located far to the north of the country in almost entirely uninhabited territories, but many of them are in the fertile valleys in southern Tibet.

The number of pilgrims varies greatly according to the time of the year. The festivals, of course, provide the greatest attraction, and on those occasions a gay and cheerful atmosphere reigns supreme,

* The Tibetan word *tshugpo* (rich) is derived from the word *tshug*, which means "cattle". So "rich" in Tibetan really means "be-cattled". This reminds one of Latin (*capita*—capital, and *pecus*—pecunia). It illustrates the importance of cattle-breeding as a means of living in Tibet.

in strange contrast to the teaching of the Buddhists, asserting that all life is inherently bad and that escaping from the wheel of rebirths and all forms of material existence is the supreme goal of the Buddhist.

Not far from the place where I had studied various meditation exercises practised by the lamas I heard that one of the famous oracles of the Tibetans, a so-called *sungmi*, was about to visit the nearest monastery and that several thousand pilgrims were flocking to the place in order to witness the demons descending to earth temporarily to take possession of the body of the oracle.

When I arrived at the monastery it was quite easy to see that something exceptional was going to happen. Large crowds of pilgrims poured into the gates from all directions. Small tradesmen had established themselves to sell food and other necessities, and there reigned an atmosphere reminding one somewhat of a good-sized fair at some Western country town. Busy-looking lamas in bright clothes moved about, and an unusually large number of temple flags and other decorations were hung out everywhere.

The demons were expected to descend into the body of the *sungmi* in the presence of a very large crowd. Moreover, the lamas had decided to provide an additional attraction by performing a religious play the following day. Theatrical performances in Tibet last much longer than in Western countries and are rehearsed most painstakingly.

From time to time the crowds moving to and fro in the narrow passages gave a good stare when one of the lamas went to the rehearsal wearing the strange robes and masks in which they were to appear in the show. Just after turning a corner I met three lamas wearing striped robes and gigantic masks hiding their faces. Each of them also had a sword in his right hand. My miniature camera, with which I could take photographs of about two-thirds of an inch by one inch, was hidden in the left sleeve of my Tibetan clothes,* and I could not resist the temptation to raise the arm a little to take a snapshot when the lamas were a few yards distant. It was a risky business, but worth the trouble, as although so small a photograph taken under such conditions seldom permits of sufficient enlargement, it is nevertheless a document of considerable scientific value.

As none of the lamas nor any of the many Tibetans filling the passage had noticed anything, I became a little bolder. A few minutes later I reached a kind of small square where a lama performing in the show had halted and was stared at curiously by a small crowd of Tibetans. He was wearing a mask representing a skull, and ribs were painted on his chest. Obviously he was intended to impersonate a walking skeleton in the show. He did not seem to be inconvenienced by the curious stares of the crowd and even posed a little so that they might examine him thoroughly. The crowd kept a respectful distance, and as the sun shone very brightly too, I could not resist the temptation to once more raise my left arm in order to take another snapshot. However, this time I had a very narrow escape. The lama and a few other Tibetans heard a

---

* It was subsequently destroyed by bandits.

faint click. The "skeleton" even made a rush towards the little crowd. But I had quietly put my arms behind my back in a natural manner. The lama walked on shaking his head, and the Tibetan crowd immediately began to talk about strange noises produced by ghosts !

Half an hour later the crowds began to move towards the central courtyard of the monastery where the *sungmi*, one of the famous oracles of the Tibetans, was to invite the demons to descend into his body in the presence of a large crowd. Although I made it a practice to avoid moving with crowds whenever I could, I realized the impossibility of isolating myself, as it was to be expected that every corner of the courtyard and the galleries would be crowded to cracking point by the several thousand pilgrims who had come to the monastery for the event, added to the many hundred lamas living there.

I had gone to the courtyard immediately after puzzling the "skeleton" lama with the click of the miniature camera, and managed to get a fairly good place right in front whence I could watch proceedings very closely. For a whole hour after this crowds continued to pour into the courtyard and the many galleries from all sides. As the time approached for the event the merry laughs and chatter of the multitude gradually gave way to breathless suspense.

Finally the *sungmi* arrived, accompanied by a large crowd of lamas of high rank, and made his entrance in a ceremonious fashion. He was middle-aged, strong and well-built, and wore bright clothes of excellent quality. He looked exceedingly prosperous. It is a fact that the *sungmi* business is

probably the one which pays best in Tibet.   Narbu,
the wealthy Tibetan with whom I made friends later
on, told me that the income of the famous *sungmis* of
Tibet equals the income of *several thousand* nomad
families.   The fee paid to a *sungmi* for one such
public sitting may equal the *annual* income of
fifty nomad families !

The oracle slowly and ceremoniously advanced
towards his seat and sat down in Occidental fashion,
but the crowd of lamas remained standing throughout the ceremony—apart from a few old lamas of
high rank who sat down in the Tibetan manner on
their *gyab-bols*.*

Bells began to ring, and a procession of priests
walked round the prosperous oracle with incense-
burners, which in most cases are made of the upper
portion of human skulls.   The suspense of the
crowd was intense and everybody was watching
the *sungmi*, who slowly lapsed into a state of
trance.   His face grew pale, his fingers crisped,
and from time to time he was shaken by convulsions from head to foot.

The great moment had arrived !   The demons
began to descend into his body.   The lamas blew
trumpets to herald their arrival.

From minute to minute the convulsions of the
oracle increased in number and amplitude.   Finally,
his whole body swayed forward and backward as
if it were pushed about by invisible entities of
extraordinary strength.

The crowd grew too excited to remain quiet.

---

* Cushions, the number of which varies according to the rank of the
lama.

Their breathless suspense gave way to occasional shouts of amazement and a strange kind of religious frenzy.

"*Lha shon*," said an old Tibetan, who stood near me.

I failed to understand him. *Lha* means god or demon, and *shon* means to ride. "The demon rides!" What could he have meant by it?

While the convulsions of the *sungmi* increased in violence and the crowd gave vent to their emotions by shouting and gesticulating, I wondered what "the demon rides" meant, and then suddenly I understood. The demon had descended into the body of the oracle to ride his body, just as does a rider who takes possession of a horse!

Now the *sungmi* had reached such a state of frenzy that a Western physician would have felt some anxiety for him. One might have been afraid that he would bite his tongue off* or fall down as the victim of a stroke. His face was dark red and swollen as if someone had wound a string round his neck to stifle him. Blood came out of his mouth, ears, and nose, and he began to groan like a wild animal.

Trumpets sounded once more, and a lama exhorted the crowd to remain silent.

The culminating part of the ceremony had begun.

The demon had entirely taken possession of the body of the *sungmi*, and the moment had come to

---

* In speaking Tibetan the tongue is very often put in between the teeth, so that many Tibetans are in the habit of continually putting their tongue in between their teeth. As a matter of fact, about six of the twenty-eight Tibetan consonants are pronounced with the tongue put in *between* the teeth.

put questions to him. Several lamas approached with loose pieces of paper on which the various questions were written. The oracle took them one by one, rubbing the slips against the crown of his head. He answered each question in a low voice audible only to the lamas surrounding him. The answer to at least one of the questions was so copiously mixed with groans that it could hardly have made any sense. The answers, however, were carefully recorded by the lamas in *all* instances. I wonder in what way they recorded the groans and what interpretation they gave to them !

The Tibetan *sungmis* are much more respected than the simple *pawos*,* who are equally able to go into a state of trance and answer questions whilst obsessed by demons.

In the opinion of the wise men of Tibet, the giving up of one's body for any purpose whatsoever to invisible entities so that they can temporarily take possession of it *is one of the greatest crimes which a human being can commit against his soul.* The Divine spark in man, his soul, is greatly offended and brutalized by them. If the soul leaves such a being such a man remains soulless for all eternity and enters the downward current of life, which leads him down again in the opposite direction, through the whole process of evolution to nothingness and total annihilation. All the horrible types of animals and plants,† they say, are incarnations of such falling entities.

The *sungmis* of Tibet must lead unnatural lives in order to retain the faculty to be obsessed by their

---

* Mediums.   † Such as snakes, toads, parasites, etc.

gods or demons.   They are not allowed to have
sexual intercourse.   They voluntarily abstain from
many amenities of life so as to be able to go on with
their business.   They must live on a special diet.
As to the food they take, I heard different stories,
but it seems that eggs and various kinds of meat are
strictly forbidden.

When only the material aspect of things is taken
into consideration, the Tibetan *sungmis* may be compared with certain patients in Western lunatic asylums
whose disease is scientifically called "dual personality".   The occultist and the materialistic nerve
specialist cannot possibly agree on these matters,
for they both approach the problem from opposite
directions.   Nerve specialists know for a fact that
in practically all cases of mental disease corresponding physical defects can be found, and for the nerve
specialist the mental trouble is a consequence of
the physical one.   The occultist takes the opposite
view.   For him the mental trouble (obsession, etc.)
is the cause and the physical trouble the result of it.
Both the nerve specialist and the occultist are right
from their angle, and it is not to be expected that
they will agree on the fundamental cause of
mental complaints.

After the *sungmi* had answered a series of questions, the spectacular part of the show began.   This
was obviously intended for the large crowds,
especially for the majority of the people who had no
possibility to get near enough to see the face of the
oracle.

A big sword was brought in by two lamas, who
appeared to be stooping under its weight.   I could

not help noting smilingly that the lamas chosen for transporting the sword were about the frailest and shortest specimens of the whole lot.   Obviously the *effect* of *two* lamas carrying a sword was calculated to impress the multitude, especially the Tibetans standing far away who were unable to see that the two lamas were very frail.

The sword was ceremoniously handed to the *sungmi*, who stood up and in a state of frenzy touched the ground with its point. He then folded the sword with his bare hands as if it had been made of hot wax.   Immediately afterwards the folded sword was carried towards the crowd, who made a mad scramble for it.   The people could ascertain that the sword weighed perhaps twenty-five pounds, and that the steel was so substantial that even the strongest man could not have bent it with his bare hands.   A substitution of the sword folded by the *sungma* by another sword was quite impossible, as the whole thing was done publicly in the presence of several thousand people.

By the way, such cases of "dual personality" in which men show an unaccountable degree of physical strength have also been studied in lunatic asylums and by occultists in Western countries.

The folding of the heavy sword seemed to put the Tibetan multitude into a state of frenzy. Crowds easily fuse into one "group soul", and then the individual no longer behaves as he would behave individually.   Crowds really are not the sum total of all the individualities present.   They seem to be a suddenly formed *new entity* actuated by a kind of "group soul".   It is man sinking back temporarily

into the "group consciousness" from which civil-
ized man is just about to emerge.   I think only the
greatest of the great, such as Shakespeare or Goethe,
were fully and definitely individualized and beyond
the possibility of lapsing back temporarily into
group consciousness.

Mild Tibetans, who would never dream of doing
such a thing individually, made a mad rush forward
to get near the *sungmi*, who still swayed to and fro
and had just begun to spit out violently in various
directions.   What an honour for the average
Tibetan to be spat at by a *sungmi* while a god or
demon was "riding" the latter !   I think he would
not forget this supreme distinction while he lived !

The maddened crowd pushed me forward towards the *sungmi*.   Women and children screamed,
and serious accidents seemed to be inevitable.   But
the Tibetan lamas are a well-organized body.   The
"police force" of the monastery put in an appearance almost immediately in the shape of about sixty
lamas of the taller and stronger variety, carrying
sticks and whips !   A minute later the crowd was
pushed back in a very energetic and ruthless manner.   The whipping lamas did their best to show off
the power of the police force.   Not even women and
children were spared by them.   I happened to be
in one of the foremost rows and tried to bow a little
—as much as I could do so in the crowd—to protect
myself from the birch whips of the police lamas, at
the same time trying hard to protect as much as
possible a beautiful young Tibetan girl standing
next to me.

When the front row had been pushed back about

twenty yards from the *sungmi* the police force retired, apparently proud and satisfied with the rapid and efficient manner in which order had been restored.

The girl had received a stroke of the whip on her hands, which she had held before her face to protect it, and although I made it a practice not to speak inside the Tibetan monasteries and posed as a deaf-and-dumb native, I departed from the practice on this special occasion, and asked her : "*Kyod zur-mo rag?*"*

She smiled, and we began to converse.

Her name was Dolma. She had come a long way from her village situated near Taratshan. She and her mother had joined a large group of *neskorpas*† and would travel back the long distance to their native village the day after tomorrow. During the row she had been separated from her mother and her friends, but would join them soon after the ceremony.

She was a very beautiful girl, and after ten minutes' conversation I found that she was remarkably clever too. Unfortunately, not all women who are beautiful are also clever. Nature often seems to hesitate to bestow too many gifts on the same individual.

She asked me my name and where I came from.

"My name is Chedi," I said, "and I have come here to stay two days to see the *sungmi* and the show to be played tomorrow."

"How many are you ?" she asked.

"I travel all alone," I answered.

She gave a merry laugh, showing her beautiful teeth perhaps a little more than was really necessary.

---

* "Do you feel pain ?" † Pilgrims.

"This is no joke," I observed. "I have told the truth—I travel alone."

"Then surely you are a *ladki*?* Only a *ladki* can do such a thing as travel quite alone. By the way, I never met a *ladki*. Do all *ladkis* talk Tibetan in such a funny manner?"

A loud blast of many dozen trumpets interrupted our conversation. The *sungmi* had ceased to move about and looked as lifeless as a corpse. His face had become like yellowish wax and was dreadful to look at.

"Would you like to meet my mother and my friends?" asked Dolma.

"No," I said.

She looked very disappointed. "Why?"

"I want *en-pa*,"† I said.

"Even when I am near you?"

"No. You are an exception." She looked very pleased.

I had a good look at her dress. Everything about her was remarkably clean, which is almost a phenomenon in Tibet.

Trumpets were blown again. After a slight pause there came a rapid succession of many blasts, a signal that the gods or demons had definitely departed.

The *sungmi* was surrounded by a large crowd of helpers. So many people brought him drink, or washed and massaged him, that it was no longer possible to see his face. Only several dozen lamas and his special suite had access to him. The crowd was still kept at a certain distance and slowly began to disperse.

---

* People from Ladakh.   † Solitude.

"Are you going back to your friends now?" I asked Dolma.

"This is not urgent, Chedi," she answered, carefully arranging her beautiful hair. "If I join them in an hour I shall be in time for our meal. Where will you stay?"

"I shall leave the monastery," I answered, "go out into the surrounding neighbourhood, and return tomorrow for the show."

"But where is your *gur*,* Chedi?"

I laughed. "It is wound round my body, and so is my blanket."

"So you carry your house wound round your body?" she remarked, laughing loudly.

"Yes, but some of my belongings are also hidden in the neighbourhood," I said.

"What a mysterious person you are!" she exclaimed.

Gradually our conversation drifted to more vital matters. For half an hour we conversed about Milaraspa, called short Mila by the Tibetans, and Padmasambhava, who wrote legends which are very different from the mild and cheerful legends of Mila and contain descriptions of horrible scenes of cannibalism and unimaginable depravities.

More and more I was amazed how much that little girl knew and how enormously she was above the educational standard of other Tibetans.

"Are there many *bu-mo-mdzes-ma*† in your village who know as much as you do?" I asked.

"Perhaps not," she said.

"Where did you learn all this?"

---

* Tent.   † Nice Tibetan girls.

"That is a secret," answered Dolma. "I have had my teachers."

"Does your mother like your teachers ?"

"She would not like them, perhaps," she said ; "but she has never met them."

"Why ?"

"She would not understand them, so I never take them home."

Dolma promised me to get away from her friends the following morning. We would then walk about for an hour or so and go together to the show in the monastery.

"Good-bye," said Dolma. "Good-bye, Chedi from—Ladakh !"

Her laugh rang out merrily. I wondered whether there had been a mocking expression in her face when she added "from Ladakh".

When we met again the following day, Dolma immediately talked about the dangers I had faced while spending the night alone in my tent at a place about ten miles from the monastery. "There are many bandits in the neighbourhood," she said. "Early this morning two solitary travellers passed our party of *neskorpas*.* They were in a pitiful plight, having been robbed of nearly all their belongings. When they were gone my mother and the other pilgrims had a good laugh about them."

"In many other countries people pity those who are robbed—or at least they pretend to do so," I observed, and at once realized the mistake of having mentioned "other countries". She did not seem to have noticed it.

---

* Pilgrims.

"My mother laughs at such people," she said. "And so do others.* But you mentioned other countries. I was in *Gyadkar*† once."

"How did you get there ?"

"I know a very powerful man," she answered. "He is very rich, perhaps one of the richest persons in the country. He lives in a splendid *dsong*.‡ He is very educated and even speaks languages other than Tibetan. I accompanied him to India two years ago."

"Are you going to marry him, Dolma ?"

"No . . . my mother is very anxious that I should meet him as often as possible, but she does not understand. . . . Narbu is a great spiritual power and I am one of his pupils."

We walked on for a few minutes without saying anything.

"Narbu is a little like you, Chedi," she went on. "He is the type of man who would sleep alone in a tent in a district infested by bandits. He is not afraid of wild animals either. Are you never attacked by animals ?"

"Seldom," I answered. "The animals which are on the rising branch of life are very kind to me. I do not think even a lion would attack me, although I never met one. I have had very pleasant experiences, though, with bears and some other so-called wild animals."

"I heard a story about a bear," said Dolma. "I will tell it to you. Perhaps you will be able to tell

---

* It is a shame in Tibet to be a victim of robbers, because the fact of having been robbed denotes a lack of cunning !

† India.   ‡ Large and expensive house.

me whether such a thing can happen. . . .   A man who often broke the law which prohibits hunting had obtained a white man's death-stick* in the Lhasa district, and when he returned to his province he went out bear-hunting.   He had shot several bears, but one day, just while he followed the track of an animal, a strong bear suddenly appeared just behind his back. . . ."

"I can quite believe this," I observed, "for bears are perhaps the most silent creatures when they move about, and they certainly can take a hunter unawares."

"Wait a moment. . . .   The hunter was so afraid when he saw the big bear just behind his back that he dropped his gun and stared aghast at the animal, who could have crushed him in a couple of seconds."

"And what happened ?" I asked.

"Well," said Dolma, "—and now comes the part of the story I had some difficulty in believing— the bear looked at the frail creature who stood tremblingly before him, his gun lying at his feet, and . . . calmly walked away."

"I can believe that," I said, "for bears have a soul, although they are only at times individualized. By the way, it is easy to say whether the hunter in the story had a soul or not."

"*Ga zug ?*"†

"If the hunter had a soul, it was impossible for him to take up the gun to shoot after the bear.   If he was soulless, he would have done so at once."

"Are there soulless animals too ?"

---

* Gun.   † "How ?"

"Oh yes. The animals on the descending branch of life are soulless."

"Which ones, for example?"

"There are many. Ravens, rats, mice—vermin, for instance."

"They behave like a soulless man?"

"Yes."

"Did these entities inhabit men before?"

"Perhaps, many thousand years ago. When they lost their soul they began to move downward."

"It is very strange. When I visited India I heard so much about progressive evolution—that life always passed upward, that the souls in minerals became souls in plants, then in animals, and after this in man, and that man finally *must* become an angel and that all this is only a question of time."

"Life would have no meaning if there was no alternative between light and darkness, Dolma," I said. "There are two currents of life. One is moving upward and the other downward. The moment one loses one's soul one is precipitated into the downward current."

"How can one lose one's soul?"

"By sinning against one's soul, Dolma."

"By a sensual life?"

"Oh no, in most cases that is a sin against one's body. You may suffer for it in this life or in some future incarnation."

"By treating others badly, then?"

"No, as a rule even this is no sin against your soul. You will get your punishment for treating others badly in this or some future incarnation, although wanton cruelty to defenceless creatures, ratlike ingratitude, or an innate tendency to spy on others already reveal a certain degree of soullessness which may be due to sins committed against one's soul in former incarnations."

"Well, then, *what* is a sin against one's soul?"

"Using spiritual things for selfish purposes. Dragging God down on earth. Trying to put one's self on a level with the Creator."

Dolma was awe-stricken.

"Then many of us here sin like that," she exclaimed.

"Yes, Dolma, but also people in other countries."

"In India?"

"Certainly."

"In *Pee-lin-pa*?"* She looked at me in a very queer way when she said that.

"Of course, there some people sin against their soul too."

"*Pee-lin-pa* must resemble Tibet in certain respects," I added after a while.

"I will tell you something interesting," said Dolma. "Narbu, my teacher, has told me that *Pee-lin-pa* is not at all one country. It is a country divided into many small provinces which often take a stand one against another."

"Really?"

"In some ways you are very similar to Narbu, Chedi, but in others—especially in spiritual matters—you do not say exactly the same things. I think he would very much like to meet you to discuss such matters."

* The country of the white people. *Peelin* really means "a being from a distant island". "Island" is translated *ling* or *lingthreng* in Tibetan.

"Where is he at present ?" I asked.

"He travels very much. He may be at home at present. A few weeks ago he returned to his *dsong* from Lhasa. He will go soon to the Valley of Mystery."

"The Valley of Mystery . . . ?"

"If you do not know what the Valley of Mystery is, I am not allowed to tell you more about it. So please do not mention it any more," she said, with a firmness which was almost startling in so young a girl.

She noticed my disappointment, smiled, and said sweetly, "But I will give you an introduction to Narbu . . . but please promise me one thing."

"What is it ?"

"When you meet Narbu, do not tell him that I mentioned to you the Valley of Mystery. I thought you knew all about it when I said that word, because you seemed to know so much about spiritual matters. . . . I am bound by a solemn oath not to speak of the Valley . . . if Narbu wants to tell you something about it he may do so, as he occupies a much higher rank in the occult fraternity."

More and more I was dumbfounded.

There is no such thing as coincidence in this world. We make chance acquaintances, but everything in our lives seems to be guided by an intricate mechanism the working of which we fail to see.

We had arrived at the central court of the monastery where the theatrical performance was to take place. It was to last many hours and the public came along, carrying a fairly large quantity of food and drink. We went on chatting and the time passed very rapidly. The Tibetans are people who

take their time. Three quarters of an hour before
the time fixed for the show the courtyard and the
galleries were already packed with people, although
the crowds were perhaps a little smaller than the
previous day, when the *sungmi* had appeared to
make a demonstration of his capacity to enter
publicly in contact with his gods or demons.

I glanced at Dolma again and again.

Was it possible that this little girl was the friend
and spiritual disciple of a rich and powerful Tibetan
who occupied a prominent position in the country,
and was a member of a powerful secret body ?

Of course, there was something about Dolma
which distinguished her enormously from any other
Tibetan girl of her age. I looked at her dress. It
was very simple and yet almost elegant. She did
not make the smallest display of ornaments, which
is a very uncommon thing amongst Tibetan women.
She was clean, which is another remarkable feature
in Tibet. She was educated and knew a lot, not
only about Tibet but also about India !

I once more looked at her fully, comparing her
with the crowd around us. It was like looking at
a duchess who had borrowed the clothes of one of
her servants and was mixing with a crowd in the
East End !

The merry chatter of the people died away. The
performance had begun.

It was very difficult for me to understand all that
was said by the actors. First of all, the classical
language used differed to some extent from colloquial Tibetan, the difference being about as great
as the one between modern English used in

business correspondence and the English in the Shakespeare folio.   Furthermore, many of the actors wore masks, which rendered understanding still more difficult.

On the other hand, however, the plot of the play was very slight.   Developments which would take perhaps three minutes on an English stage were drawn out into scenes lasting sometimes forty minutes !   Moreover, the dialogue was supported by enormous gestures enabling even people seated at a considerable distance to guess developments. Taking all in all, I could understand a great deal.

The play glorified renunciation and non-resistance to evil.   Again and again it stressed the prospect of getting *happiness* as a reward for renunciation.

The hero of the play (I use the word in a technical sense, for a pitiful hero he was for that matter) was out to discard his personality *in order to get happiness*.

Why do people seek an unselfish conception of life ?

Is it because we have so much love and sympathy with the troubles of others that we begin to be ashamed of our selfishness which causes so much suffering ?

Or is it because we want *happiness* in exchange for a non-egocentrical conception of life ?

In the play performed in the monastery the motive of the hero was the latter and not the former.   He wanted bliss as a reward for discarding his personality.

The play started with an exceedingly long monologue on the evils of existence.   I quote from memory.   The taking down of notes while I travelled in disguise in Tibet was most difficult and only possible on rare occasions.

The hero in the play dwelt at great length on the various evils of existence. He seemed to lose sight of the many things which make life worth living and which are partly even within the reach of people not specially favoured by fortune, such as love, friendship, enthusiasm, beauty of nature, etc.

"Life is bad," he mused,
"Life is suffering and pain only.
"Nothing is real.
"Everything is unreal.
"Annihilation is the goal."

I looked at beautiful Dolma. I looked at the sun generously filling with his radiant light the court-yard of the monastery, and wondered whether the poor hero realized what dreadful blasphemy he was uttering.

What! The Creator should have made this wonderful universe—full of suffering, true, but also full of enjoyment, the suffering preventing enjoyment from becoming monotonous—for the purpose that His creatures should realize that existence was an evil and that their supreme goal was to escape from it!

I compared the poor hero in the Tibetan play with the glorious figure of Hamlet, who intensely feels the dreadful tragedy of being only a man and nothing but man. Being a genius and capable of the most intense feelings, Hamlet suffers infinitely more than the Tibetan hero, but nevertheless he has the courage and nobility of character to face his troubles as a creature without any thought of escape or "salvation".

The hero was married and had children. He worked to feed his family.

He was attacked by a swarm of mosquitoes.

The lamas had a strange stage trick to represent an enormous swarm of mosquitoes. I wondered how it was done, but it looked very genuine.

The hero gave his life-blood to the mosquitoes! "The dear little ones," he said, "let them have a good meal. I have to feed my family, but the family and the mosquitoes are the same thing!"

Having fed so many mosquitoes, the hero was taken ill and the play went on, describing his sufferings and the sufferings of his family brought about by his inability to work.

Just when their food supply was running out, rats put in an appearance in their house. The part of rats was played by Tibetan children who wore masks and neatly carried their long tails under their arms. The hero said :

"Eat, little rats, eat, eat, eat,
"Feed your little bodies, grey brothers.
"Eat, grey brothers, eat, eat, eat.
"Our food is yours, grey brothers.
"Eat, little rats, eat, eat, eat."

I quote these passages from memory, but should like to add that the text of the dialogues and mono-logues was much longer, and much more elaborate.

The rats ate the food of the semi-starved family and became more and more numerous.

A scene came in now in which the hero exalted the happiness of giving away everything. "If the rats eat the first half of my meal, I give them the second half," he exclaimed, in what a heretical spectator might have called a fit of religious hysteria.

He did not seem to consider what his own children thought of it, but this seemed to be of less importance to him than the well-being of the rats.

All the above had lasted more than two hours, but the play went on uninterruptedly—the Tibetan crowds following it with breathless suspense. Some people had their mouths wide open, while others shed tears, and not a whisper could be heard.

In the following scene the rats had become fourfold in number. All the food was eaten. The hero and his children were seated in the centre and a few dozen rats walked round them in circles which were becoming smaller and smaller.

"*Kyir*, *kyir*.* We are hungry. Round, round, round. There is nothing to eat, *kyir*, *kyir*, *kyir*," came the chorus of the rats.

The hero started a long monologue full of pity for the rats. The religious gentleman seemed to have forgotten all about the hunger of his own children.

Suddenly the rats seized one of the children and carried the little one outside in order to devour it. The hero was unperturbed. He started a lofty monologue about the joy of sacrificing one's own children and the glory of union of all creatures.

At that moment a Tibetan youngster stifled a laugh. The public was aghast and there were loud shouts of protest. The sinner was instantly escorted

---

* "Round, round."

out by a few lamas and the play went on. It was some time before a few old ladies had got over their indignation.

Dolma told me in whispers that she could not remember having seen a play where the "religious" tendency had been so apparent as in the present one.

The amusement of the Tibetan youngster had greatly upset the lamas. Dolma said that it was probable they would quickly cancel a few of the remaining scenes which were "most religious", as the play seemed to be too strong for the younger generation.

"Have you ever seen so highly religious a play ?" she asked in a low voice.

"No," I said. I am sure I told the truth when I said that.

The monologue of the hero, which had been interrupted by the outbreak of the youngster, continued interminably. He envied his child, he declared, because it had for a short while at least made its escape from this world of suffering.

He seemed to imply that death was a very cheerful and enviable process.

After finishing his monologue, the hero was distinctly pleased. So were the rats. And the religious play went on. As I learned later, it was somewhat in the nature of an experiment, and the lamas had actually got together to cancel a few scenes to prevent a recurrence of the irreverent incident and the dreadful calamity of another stifled laugh.

I knew that the lamas seldom fail to introduce themselves and a certain number of demons into

religious plays performed in Tibetan monasteries. I
was waiting anxiously for their appearance, as the
endless monologues and dialogues had become
rather tedious.

Finally a lama appeared in the show. He had
obviously been chosen and dressed in a way calculated to show the Tibetan priesthood in the best
possible light. Moreover, everything the lama
said in the play seemed to be intended to strengthen
the authority of the priests. The lama did not give
many explanations to the devout and respectful
hero, but insisted on blind *belief*. The latter repeated
on several occasions :

"I believe you, O lama.
"Yes, I believe you.
"Yes, yes, yes, I believe you.
"I do not disbelieve you, O lama.
"No, I do not disbelieve you.
"No, no, no, I do not disbelieve you."

The hero explained to the lama that he had
sacrificed everything in order to attain the joys of
Nirvana. He enumerated his merits in a fashion
none too modest. He had even given his own
children to feed those poor darling rats. But he
was worried about the sins he had committed before
embarking on his virtuous existence. That was
why he requested the spiritual assistance and
advice of the holy lama, who deigned to meet him
in a lofty spirit of sacrifice and pity for this sinful
world which was so greatly in need of lamas to fight
evil and to take a stand for :

"Encouragement to be good.
"Admonition to avoid evil.
"Advice to clean the heart.
"Such as is the Law of the Buddhist."

If my memory serves me correctly, the last two verses were even textually borrowed from Sanskrit and pronounced by the actor in that language with a strong Tibetan accent :
"*Sa chittaparyo dapanam,*
"*Etam Buddhāna sāsanam.*"
The following is a synopsis of the subsequent conversation between the sinner and the lama freely translated from the lofty and complicated language used by the Tibetan actors into simple and intelligible English :

Sinner : "I am glad you are here to advise me."
Lama : "What can I do for you ?"
Sinner : "I have sinned very badly in earlier life."
Lama : "It does not matter. I am *glad* you sinned then."
Sinner : "What ! You—a *holy man*—are *glad* that I sinned ?"
Lama : "Yes, I am glad you sinned, because there is more joy for three sinners who repent than for three hundred people who need not repent because they have never sinned."

I could not help thinking that under such conditions it is really a fine thing to sin, because there is more joy about sinners who repent than about the permanently virtuous !

Finally, demons began to put in an appearance in the show. It seemed to be interminable. By now we had been seated at least four hours and the performance still went on.

"O lama, give me religion."

"Give me religion, O lama," exclaimed the sinner pathetically again and again.

In the following scene a few demons appeared in the background. This did not seem to hasten developments in any way. The plot of the play seemed exceedingly slight.

I looked at Dolma. She appeared rather bored and did not attempt to hide the fact. "Shall we go ?" I whispered.

"It is a little *kar-wa** to get away without attracting attention," she answered. "And then, my mother and the other members of my party are scattered all over the audience."

"We need not walk out together," I suggested.

"Well," said the girl, "I shall walk out first and wait for you just beyond the western gate of the monastery. I am going at once . . . so at the western gate of the monastery." She repeated it with great care and left immediately, stooping a little and taking a zigzag course across the crowd.

A few minutes later I followed her.

There is no country in the world where people are more interested in religious matters than they are in Tibet. Religion plays a very important part in everyday conversation, although few people are interested in really deep religious problems, talks of sorcery, divination, and alleged miracles being much

---

* Difficult.

more frequent than theological discussions. However, Dolma seemed to have a bent for the latter.

She asked me whether I considered the attitude of the hero in the play a proper one for a really religious person.

"No," I answered.

"Shall man be selfish, then?" she asked. "Is it wrong to try to be good?"

"No, but it is wrong to try to be like God."

"But God is good. Trying to be like God leads to goodness."

"The creature must not overstep its limits," I said, "by trying to be like God. If he does so, he acts like the angels who revolted against the Creator. There are two different types of impersonality—namely, Be-ing and Be-ness.* The former is an attribute of the creature, the latter an attribute of the Creator.

Be-ness is absolute impersonality where *all* division between the "I" and the "non-I" ceases. It is beyond the reach of the creature.

"What happens to a man who wants to attain this state?" asked Dolma.

"He commits the greatest and most deadly sin against the Creator.

She looked greatly perturbed and changed the topic.

"Are you leaving today, Chedi?" she asked.

"Yes, Dolma," I answered. "Are you?"

"We shall ride back in the direction of Taratshan. . . . What a pity that you cannot come along."

---

* *Sat* in Sanscrit. This subtle difference cannot be expressed in any Western language.

"But Taratshan is almost the same direction which I intended to take, Dolma."

She did not make any attempt to hide her joy.

"Splendid !" she exclaimed. "You may follow us on horseback, and we can meet every day in the evening when the members of my party have retired. But we have good horses and ride about thirty miles a day."*

"That is a very good plan," I said. "What does your horse look like ?"

She gave an accurate description of it. Then she asked, "And yours ? You never mentioned it."

"I do not need a horse, Dolma," I said.

She thought I had made a joke.

"I am quite serious," I added. "I can *walk* at least thirty miles a day."

"So can I," she said, "but only a day or two. You can't walk one hundred and twenty miles in four days."

"I can," I said, and she believed me. I then briefly explained that I did without a horse to keep in form in order to be able to traverse territories where horses cannot be used.

It was arranged that I should leave the district before Dolma. She and her party would leave two hours later and overtake me about noon the following day. I already mentioned earlier in the book that vision in most parts of Tibet is excellent. We also devised a very simple and efficient method of marking the places we were passing. I should

---

* In most parts of Tibet this is an exceptionally good daily average to cover on horseback. There are practically no roads and the ground is often sandy.

have no difficulty in finding the place where they would put up their tents. An hour or two after nightfall I was to howl twice like a wolf. Dolma would then leave her tent and join me for some time.

"Are you certain that they will let you get away alone so late?" I asked.

"Yes," she answered. "I am very resourceful. By the way, I inhabit one half of the tent of my mother separated by a partition from the other half. No one is permitted to enter my 'room' under any circumstances unless I call. Even my mother does not do it. So I shall crawl out and try to get past the man keeping watch. Should he see me, I shall tip him to keep his mouth shut."

She also promised to write out a letter of introduction addressed to Narbu and to hand it to me in the evening together with an exact description of the place where his *dsong* was located.

"And now I must meet my party again," she said, when we returned to the gate of the monastery. "The show is nearly over."

I walked about alone in order to think. How crowded those two days had been! The demons taking possession of the body of the *sungmi*; my meeting a beautiful and clever Tibetan girl who was about to introduce me to a powerful man belonging to an influential secret society; a genuine theatrical performance in a Tibetan monastery in all probability never before visited by any white person—all this I had observed and experienced within a period of less than two days!

I then collected my food supply and started in the direction indicated by beautiful little Dolma.

CHAPTER III

DOLMA and her party on horseback overtook me early in the afternoon. By the little signs imperceptibly dropped by Dolma every few hundred yards at regular intervals I could easily find the place where the party had put up their tents.

I waited until about two hours after nightfall and then howled twice like a wolf. Dolma heard the signal and a quarter of an hour later she had joined me in the darkness.

"Has someone seen you leave ?" I asked.

"Yes," she answered. "I could not get away without being noticed by the night-watchman who has to be on the look-out for brigands. But I promised him a bag of barley-meal if he will keep his mouth shut.

"As soon as I had done this I ran away as fast as Pal-Dorjee to come here," she added.

"Who is Pal-Dorjee ?" I asked.

"What," she exclaimed, "you do not know who Pal-Dorjee was ?"

"No," I said.

Dolma looked at me in a strange way. As I learnt later, there is hardly a Tibetan—including the less-educated ones—who has never heard the story of Pal-Dorjee, a Tibetan who committed a pious

72

murder at the epoch corresponding to our Middle Ages.

Pal-Dorjee was a clever and resourceful fellow. When he was "wanted" and his pursuers hounded him to a Tibetan village, he quickly stole a horse, blackened it with soot, and galloped away, his pursuers following him on other horses. When he arrived at a river Pal-Dorjee swam across, but while his horse crossed the river the soot was washed away and the animal had turned white by the time they arrived on the opposite bank ! When the pursuers arrived at the river they saw a man gallop away on the other side on a *white* horse. So these mediaeval "cops" thought that Pal-Dorjee had disappeared, and returned home !

Dolma had brought a lot of food from her tent. Surely women are alike everywhere. They never lose sight of the physical well-being of someone in whom they are interested.

She opened her food parcel, and when I refused to take meat our conversation at once turned to vegetarianism.

"Why do you dislike *sha** ?" she asked.

"I do not dislike it," I answered.

"Then why don't you eat it ?"

"Because I find it coarse to eat meat. If I eat a piece of meat I feel like someone who would bite into his left arm to eat it."

"There are some people who never eat meat," said Dolma, "but I do not like them. They seem to be *afraid* of eating meat."

"Here again, you see, Dolma, that it is really

---

* Meat.

more important *why* we do things than *what* we are doing."

We chatted for half an hour and then Dolma returned to her *gur*.*

I spent the night in my tent and started half an hour before sunrise. The party again overtook me later on in the day at a distance of about half a mile. I slightly modified my direction and followed the little signs dropped regularly by the Tibetan girl.

We met again long after sunset in the same manner as the day before.

Dolma told me that the "watchdog" had come to collect his tip in the morning and when he had got it he had gone to her mother, telling her all he knew about her absence the preceding night, thus securing a second tip. Her mother had been angry and she had told a lie about a solitary walk she had taken during the night. However, this evening she had escaped entirely unnoticed by another Tibetan who had kept watch during the night.

"Narbu, my teacher, has always told me that a spiritual person should never tell a lie," she said. "I feel guilty, but fail to see how human society can be kept going without lies."

"There are people who say things which are untrue," I observed, "but it is infinitely worse if someone misrepresents facts and creates a wrong impression without telling a real and formal lie. Such a thing is devilish and greatly offends the Creator much more in fact than an outright lie."

"I think you are right," observed Dolma. "I

---

* Tent.

know a story about an occurrence in a monastery which shows how a man can lie against the spirit without telling a real and formal lie.

"A Tibetan went to confess his sins to a lama whom he knew very well. Just before he entered the monastery he found a valuable object which he knew was the private property of the lama to whom he was going to confess his sins. He showed it to the priest, but the latter was absent-minded and without looking at it said, 'I do not want it.' Then confession started. The Tibetan asked what he should do if he found a valuable object lying on the ground. 'You must hand it to the rightful owner,' said the lama, 'and if he cannot be found immediately, to the monastery.' 'And if the rightful owner does not want it?' asked the Tibetan. 'Then you may keep it,' said the lama.—The Tibetan left the monastery and kept the valuable object. He knew he had not sinned and had not told a single lie."

We both laughed heartily.

"Although this lie was no formal lie at all, I much prefer your innocent lying, Dolma," I observed.

Is it not a fact that the more man penetrates into the realm of spirituality the more he is apt to lose himself in a tangle of things where words and formal standards of value cease to be a reliable basis, and where everything may be conveniently used as an excuse?

The following evening Dolma and I met for the last time. The day afterwards her party had reached their village.

It was not until the parting hour that I fully

realized how greatly this beautiful Tibetan girl was devoted to me. She herself may have thought that it was a kind of "soul love", but perhaps she was deceiving herself. It was, no doubt, soul love, but soul love with a very pronounced human touch. No matter how much human relationships are on so-called "higher" levels, there is always a personal touch in them. It may be latent, but is nevertheless very real.

There are, no doubt, spiritual people among my readers who profoundly disagree with me in this connection and who stick to the opinion that "spiritual" contacts must be free from any "lower" human element. To these readers I should recommend to put to themselves the question whether it would not have mattered at all if Dolma had been a woman of, say, seventy years of age (there are some women of that age who are still very spiritual and vital), or if Dolma, the beautiful young girl, had met me in the visible form of a very spiritual and vital old man of the apparent age of eighty.

The next few days were somewhat uneventful until I reached the Tibetan *dsong** in which Narbu, Dolma's spiritual teacher, lived. I looked forward to my interview with him. After all that Dolma had told me about him he appeared not only a highly spiritual person, but also someone entrusted with an important political mission by the Occult Brotherhood to which he belonged.

During the next few days I suffered greatly from lack of water for drinking and washing. There had been no rainfall for many days and everything

* Large house built for powerful people.

in the district had dried up rapidly. However, an individual accustomed to travel alone in the various deserts of the world easily adapts himself to difficult situations. Even half a pint of water can last over long distances if you merely use it for wetting your parched lips and then put about a cubic inch of water into your mouth, swallowing it very slowly, almost drop by drop. In this way half a pint of water may keep one going for two days.

The last afternoon before I reached Narbu's *dsong* there was a violent thunderstorm. Something like two inches of rain fell in half an hour. Just before the thunderstorm set in, the sky looked indescribably majestic. It was a sight such as can be seen only once in many years in western countries. The clouds were almost as black as ink and looked as if demons of gigantic proportions were brewing something in a cauldron. Some of the clouds resembled gigantic monsters, and when the torrential downpour started, sheets of lightning followed one another at the rate of about three sheets per second.

Narbu's *dsong** was situated in a comparatively densely inhabited area. I usually avoided the trade routes while I travelled in disguise in Tibet and gave an especially wide berth to places where I had reason to believe that white people had put in an appearance. If my information was correct, the various District Governors in Tibet were by then for the most part connected by telephone lines,

---

* The Tibetan word "*dsong*" has a double meaning. It means fortress or seat of a District Governor. But it also means a private residence inhabited by rich people.

which, by the way, seems to indicate that the Tibetans do pin a little more faith on those new-fangled things imported for long-distance communication from the West than on their sorcerers, who are supposed to be able to send messages "on the wind"—as the Tibetans put it—that is to say, by telepathy.

To have been found at a place serving as a residence to a *dsongpön** would have been a terrific experience in the forbidden country, and it was highly probable that the place in which Narbu resided had been chosen as a place of residence by such an individual.

To minimize the risk of detection I spent the last night a long distance away from the place and then walked ten miles non-stop early in the morning, intending to arrive at Narbu's residence about an hour and a half after sunrise.

Even then I narrowly escaped trouble.

When the first houses came in view I sat down for a little while in order to take a few minutes' rest before approaching the residence. While I sat there a Tibetan left one of the houses and came up to the place where I was seated on the ground.

He eyed me suspiciously as if he had been the Tibetan equivalent of a plain-clothes man and then asked in a none too friendly way :

"*Tshi la iru dug?*"†

"*Na shrun te dad,*"‡ I answered in as natural a way as possible, a slight touch in my voice denoting a mild degree of annoyance at being disturbed.

---

* District Governor.   † "What are you doing here ?"
‡ "I sit here to watch."

There was nothing particular to be watched. The man once more eyed me suspiciously and went away, but when I arrived at Narbu's house a few minutes later I noticed that he had shadowed me. Police methods are frightfully primitive in Tibet.

When he saw that I handed a letter to a servant of so respectable and powerful a man he seemed to be reassured and walked away. The *gla-mi** looked at my cheap *chu-pa*† in a none too respectful way. The humbler the position of a man in life the more he is inclined to value a man by such futilities as dress and similar trifles, and Tibet does not seem to be different from the West in this respect. He told me that he would hand the letter to "His Excellency", but when I said I had to wait for an answer he turned a deaf ear to my request and went away.

I waited patiently for half an hour, a wait which was not very pleasant, since some of the passers-by seemed to eye me rather curiously while I stood there in my poor clothes before the main entrance of the rich man's *dsong*.

Suddenly a man of about fifty years of age, dressed in pure silk, came out of the house. He at once apologized in a very courteous and apparently sincere manner for having kept me waiting. Dolma's letter, he explained, had only been handed to him a few minutes before and he had severely reprimanded the servant for having taken things so leisurely. The Tibetan "Excellency", who seemed to be a perfect gentleman, then led me upstairs,

---

* Servant.   † Gown.

to the amazement of the servant who had taken my letter.

The floors were covered with costly *gdans** and everything in the house seemed to be well-appointed and very clean.

"Dolma has written a very long *yige*,†" said Narbu, while we walked together to the room where breakfast was served. "She is a clever girl and seldom makes a mistake in judging people. She writes that you seem to be a man who possesses a very independent outlook on spiritual matters and is a determined truth-seeker. I always liked such people. Dolma also writes that you have travelled very much and that she has some difficulty to believe that you are Tibetan or Ladakhi at all. Would you not make a clean breast of it? Neither Dolma nor I ever betray anyone. You have my word of honour that nothing whatsoever which you may entrust to me will ever leak out."

I looked at him and was more and more impressed by his unostentatious attitude and sincere manner.

A servant entered the room, bringing various kinds of food. It was the first time during my travels in Tibet that I had something almost amounting to what may be called an opulent breakfast. I even got *Shogri* from India and other things which are considered great delicacies by the Tibetans.

The servant left the room, and Narbu once more told me that it would be better for all concerned if I did not hide from him anything.

"I shall tell you the truth," I said, "but Your

---

* Carpets.   † Letter.

Excellency will be greatly and perhaps unpleasantly surprised."

"Drop the 'Excellency'," he said smilingly. "Dolma's friends are my own, and spiritual ties remove all considerations of rank.   Let us be friends."

The servant returned with more food. As soon as he opened the door we began to talk about meaningless things, Narbu asking whether I had heard any interesting things on my travels.

I answered that I had seen and heard very much during the last few weeks.

Suddenly the servant almost opened his mouth with amazement. What was the matter? I realized that I had committed the dreadful crime of using the words "*mthon*" and "*thos*"* in answering His Excellency, instead of employing the more polite and ceremonial words "*gzigs*" and "*gsan*", which mean exactly the same thing.

The servant looked greatly puzzled. Narbu asked him whether he had something else to attend to in the room, and when the *gla-mi*† answered in the negative, Narbu ordered him to put tea and tea-cups in the study and then to join the *zas-gner*‡ and not to return before the time had come for the next meal.

We went to Narbu's study, and when we had sat down I broke the news to him that I was a Westerner travelling in disguise.

"I had my suspicions the moment I saw you," he replied smilingly, "but you played your part

---

* "Seen" and "heard".   † Servant.
‡ The chief cook of his household.

remarkably well.   Unless people's attention is specially drawn to you I doubt whether even educated Tibetans would find you out."

"I have decided to turn deaf and dumb every time I meet lamas or educated people," I told him.

"That is a very wise course to take," he observed. "Do not feel uncomfortable because I told you that I had felt the unTibetan atmosphere about you.   I have travelled extensively, both on private business and on behalf of my friends in the Valley.   I have been to India, China, Japan, and Peelinpa. We may speak English if you like."

The lengthy conversations which followed were in English until we took our next meal, during which we were attended by two servants. Narbu had a fairly good knowledge of English.

Our talk drifted to the subject of politics and the various Great Powers.   Narbu seemed to have excellent—although in some respects a little stale— information about the currents underlying the various visible political trends of our time. We soon felt that our conversation was of the greatest mutual benefit.

He once more assured me that neither he nor Dolma would ever betray me and that I should communicate with him immediately in case I got into trouble.   "My arms are very long in this country," he added smilingly.

Again he casually mentioned the "Valley". While we talked about other matters, he again and again mentioned a valley in Tibet where many highly evolved spiritual people lived with whom he was in close contact. When he mentioned it for the fourth time I took this for an invitation to ask him something about it.

I then learned that the Valley of Mystery was the headquarters of a powerful Occult Fraternity of which Narbu was a member. Dolma had never visited it.

"Are you interested in such things?" he asked me bluntly, since I maintained a certain reserve every time he began to go more fully into the matter.

"Yes," I answered, "I am interested in all spiritual matters, but I never join any sect or association whatsoever."

"Why?" he asked.

"Because I wish to maintain absolute independence," I answered.

"In our Fraternity the freedom of the members is always respected," he observed. "Spiritual freedom is our guiding principle."

"Have you a chief?" I asked.

"Yes. He is very great, perhaps the greatest power on earth. But our members obey him voluntarily."

"Why is it called the 'Valley of Mystery'?" I asked.

"This is the name given to it by the multitude," he answered. "No one except our members and occasional guests are admitted to the Valley, and the population does not know much about it and people who live in the same district even abstain from talking about it. That is why it is commonly called the 'Valley of Mystery'."

"How about the guests who occasionally visit the Valley?" I asked. "By whom are they invited?"

"The members who hold a somewhat higher position in the Occult Hierarchy may invite guests, but then they are entirely and personally responsible for them. I happen to be such a member," stated Narbu.

"What obligations must a guest enter into before he is allowed to visit the Valley?" I asked him.

"None at all. Until he joins the Fraternity he is under no obligation at all."

"But what qualifies a man to be chosen as such a guest?"

"A sincere and whole-hearted desire for salvation," said Narbu.

"Do you think I am such a man?"

"I think you are. If you care to come, I shall invite you on my own responsibility."

Then and there he fetched a rough sketch-map of Tibet.

"The only obligation for you," he said, while he put the map on the carpet before us, "is an undertaking that you will not reveal its exact location."

I promised this and he immediately showed me on the map the location of the Valley.

"I propose that you should leave early tomorrow morning. I shall give instructions to one of my servants to accompany you until the evening so that you may get away from this district, where all strangers are regarded with some suspicion. I shall also give you a letter stating that you are a member of my household. If you are annoyed by officials or lamas, show them the letter."

Narbu drank the contents of another cup of tea. During the last half-hour he had gulped down the contents of one cup after another at the rate of one cup every five minutes. And good-sized cups they were too. He added sugar every time. Only very rich Tibetans can afford such a thing. Since sugar is expensive in comparison with the income of the Tibetan multitude, the Tibetans in the humble walks of life do not add sugar to their tea. Even on the rare occasions when they do not mix it with butter and barley-meal, they do not dissolve the sugar in the tea but merely touch it from time to time with the tip of their tongue, washing down the liquid at intervals.

"This is the ninth cup since you came here," observed Narbu. "Has it ever occurred to you that nine is a very auspicious number?"

"I have studied the various occult philosophies," I answered, "and have my own views on numerology which are the result of much independent thinking. I do not hold the view that nine is an auspicious number."

"Why?"

"I think man ought not to carry numerological speculations beyond the figure five," I answered.

"Why that?"

"Five is the number of man. The higher numbers lead to complication and perdition, the smaller ones to God."

"But surely the number nine exists!"

"It does, because the conventional system of counting runs up to nine, and then ten quite arbitrarily becomes the higher unit. We could just as well adopt a system in which we should have only four figures, namely one, two, three, four—five being equivalent to the higher unit. Then nine would not exist, nor would six, seven and eight, which in my opinion—arithmosophically—are all numbers of complication, entanglement, and seduction."

"What an original idea!" exclaimed Narbu. "I have studied numerology* for several years. Its occult bearing is enormous. Figures have an occult connection with abstract notions with which we co-relate them. In this way figures can be made a kind of medium between the Divine and man."

"Numerology is a highly double-edged affair," I observed, "although it looks quite harmless."†

"Suppose we get down to concrete numerological notions," said Narbu. "Although you seem to be reluctant to indulge in numerological abstractions beyond the figure five, perhaps you will have no objection to our taking up one, two, three, four and five. Take one: one is the number of oneness—the number of non-manifested Divinity. I think you must agree to this."

"Yes," I observed, "I do. If we imagine a point in space, it is a mere abstraction, for a point really is immaterial. So one is the number of undivided abstract existence."

"I am surprised that you introduce geometrical notions into the field of numerology. It is a very original idea," observed Narbu. "Now let us take

* The philosophy of abstract figures.
† The following conversation on numerology has a connection with some of the observations made by the author in the mysterious Underground City of the Initiates described later in the book.

the figure two. It represents the contrast between spirit and matter."

"I profoundly disagree with you here," I said.

"Do you deny that two is the number of contrasts?" asked Narbu, greatly surprised.

"I agree that two is the number of contrasts," I answered, "but not *the* contrast you have just mentioned. If we take two points in space, they determine the position of a straight line, which also is immaterial. But it remains to be seen *what* abstract contrast is reflected by the figure two. You say it is the one between spirit and matter. In my opinion you are wrong. Spirit is an abstraction but matter is not. So the abstract line represented by figure two which connects two points, each of which is immaterial, really is the contrast *between two different kinds of spirit* and not between spirit and matter."

Narbu remained silent for a while and then he said, "You seem to be right; but this never occurred to me. More and more I feel how useful you would be to us in the Secret City in the Valley of Mystery."

For the first time he had mentioned a secret city.

"There must be *two altogether different types of spirituality* which are diametrically opposed to each other," I continued. "That, in my opinion, is the numerological significance of the figure two."

We then discussed three and four, and agreed that three was the dynamic number *par excellence* and four the number of matter. Three points scattered in space determine the position of a triangle, I observed, but only four abstract points lay down the outline of a geometrical form having corporeal existence. With three therefore we leave the realm of the abstract and with four we enter the domain of the concrete. Four is the number of the visible universe, the number of matter.

"We have not yet reached the *dangerous figures*," said Narbu smilingly.

"If we imagine five points scattered in space," I went on, "and call them A, B, C, D and E, we may envisage A, B, C and D only and obtain a geometrical form. But we may also link up A, B, C and E, and obtain another geometrical form. In fact we can obtain five different combinations, namely, ABCD, ABCE, ABDE, ACDE and BCDE. Five therefore represents the *interpenetration of five different spaces*. With five the creature has reached the very limits of its existence. Five is the number of the creature and the number of manifested life which seems to exist simultaneously on five planes. Man lives, if I may say so, in five different realms, viz., the physical one and those of sensation, feeling, intelligence, and will. These are five realms which interpenetrate each other.

"If you imagine six points scattered in space," I went on, "a synthetical geometrical conception of the various connections between the six points is obviously *beyond the reach of man*. As I said before, the figures exceeding five—viewed numerologically —have a dissociating effect on the personality of man. They are numbers of perdition."

Narbu was in deep thought.

"You have taught me much during these few

minutes," he observed after a while. "It is good sometimes to hear about conceptions which are very different from the ones to which we are accustomed. By the way, can you give me a short definition of what matter really is?"

"Matter," I replied, "may be regarded as the battle-ground on which two different types of spirituality fight each other."

"That is where we disagree again," observed Narbu. "I always thought that there was only *one* type of spirituality."

"I think this is a question to be decided by experience rather than by argument," I said.

"We shall discuss this further in the Secret City," observed Narbu.

For the second time he had hinted at the existence of a Secret City.

He proceeded to show me the various parts of his house. He also had a large garden which must have been quite an extraordinary thing in the district, since parks and gardens are but seldom to be found in Tibet outside the Lhasa district. He was very friendly, and said that he greatly appreciated my company. I felt that he was absolutely sincere, and that he did not "act" in any way.

A servant came up to him announcing two visitors of rank, and went away to show them into a kind of elegantly furnished reception-room.

"It will perhaps be better for you not to talk to them," observed Narbu. "I suggest that you wait for me here, and if my absence becomes lengthy you may go up to my study to the library or to the garden."

His Excellency smiled and went to the reception-room.

A high Tibetan official passed me a few seconds later, led by a servant and accompanied by a Tibetan officer. When he saw my cheap *chu-pa** he eyed me with obvious contempt, as he did not know, of course, that I was Narbu's guest; but when the door of the reception-room was opened by another servant his attitude of haughty arrogance suddenly gave way to toadlike obsequiousness as he greeted Narbu, who had come to the threshold to meet him.

When the visitors had left, Narbu joined me immediately, and soon afterwards a substantial meal was served, including such delicacies as potatoes, rice and apples, which are practically never eaten by the Tibetan multitude because they are much too expensive. Again and again another servant brought a silver dish containing tepid water for washing our fingers.

After dinner we went to the library. Although most books were Tibetan, of course, there were quite a few English books in it, including fairly recent works on occultism and political and sociological questions.

"Is there also a library in the Valley of Mystery?" I asked him.

"Yes," he replied, "but it is only accessible to the members of the Fraternity. You are going there as my guest—on my full and personal responsibility —but guests are not allowed to visit the library of the Forbidden City unless they obtain special

* Gown.

permission which only the chief of the Occult Hierarchy, whom we reverently call the Prince of Light, can grant."

Narbu drew a sketch and then handed it to me, saying :

"This sketch shows you the best way to reach the Valley. Will you permit me to add some money for your expenses during the journey ?" He took a bundle of new Tibetan banknotes* and a handful of silver coins out of a drawer.

"No," I said, "it is very kind of you, but I travel alone and meet brigands from time to time. It is of no use for me to take so much money along, as it would almost certainly be taken away on the next occasion I meet them. I still have some coins which are carefully hidden in my shoes. I cannot take more."

"I am sorry," said Narbu ; "but I notice your shoes are no longer in good condition. If you permit me to loan you a new and comfortable pair of leather shoes and a new *chu-pa* I should be very, very pleased."

I then spent the larger part of the afternoon in the library.

After the substantial evening meal served by three servants and another walk in the garden, Narbu led me to one of the guest-rooms situated on the first floor. I then spent a few hours in repairing my equipment and tried to fall asleep a couple of hours after sunset—which is a very difficult matter

---

* For about ten years past the Tibetan Government has issued bank-notes which, however, are currency only in the less isolated districts of the country.

in the inhabited part of Tibet, since most Tibetans show just as little consideration for people who may want to fall asleep as the inhabitants of some parts of the continent of Europe. Since Narbu's *dsong* was surrounded by many Tibetan houses the various noises went on unabated until late at night.

At five o'clock in the morning, kind-hearted and hospitable Narbu rose personally to see to it that I was properly attended to by the servants, and after an early breakfast taken in the company of my host, I left his *dsong* accompanied by one of his trusted servants, who had instructions to accompany me until I had left the inhabited district.

Before I left, Narbu told me that he would leave his house for the Valley of Mystery on horseback a day or two later, and he handed me a letter of introduction. He added that he had already sent a message announcing my arrival to the City of the Initiates by a messenger on horseback, who had left the *dsong* the previous day.

.   .   .   .   .

After Narbu's servant had left me to return to the *dsong* of his master I had only one experience worth recording before I reached the Valley of Mystery.

The following day I came across a group of Tibetan ascetics who believed that it was possible to attain spiritual results by fasting and other exercises having a direct influence on the body.

Their belief was briefly as follows :

Man is both spirit and matter. Spirit is immanent. It is immovable and Divine by its very essence. So all man has to do is to attend to the channel through which spirit manifests itself, namely his body, and thus the flow of spirit will pass through it without hindrance and man will become automatically spiritualized !

These *gnen-dnas* ascetics fasted, and during the course of their fast and other physical exercises, destined to keep their bodies absolutely pure, they were, of course, intensely conscious of their bodies. Their exercises really seemed to amount to a strange kind of dissociation of man's consciousness by concentrating all his awareness into his body.

It was a most unusual experience to meet people in Tibet who took so great care of their bodies. Painstaking care for them seemed to be a kind of fixed idea with this special type of ascetics. They considered butter as not pure enough for cleaning their bodies* and replaced it by mustard and oil, the price of which is much more than the Tibetan multitude can afford.

If someone concentrates his whole attention on his body and in doing so uses various choice things —the price of which is exorbitant—it is small wonder that he is more selfish in his everyday life than the ordinary individual who does not turn the care of his body into a religion. These *gnen-dnas* ascetics are not very numerous, and provide

---

* The usual way of cleaning one's body in Tibet is by rubbing it with a pat of butter. Many a reader will no doubt smile at this, but the author has found that butter really has an excellent cleaning effect on the body. Soap has been used in the West only during the last few centuries, and the ancient Romans, who were very clean people, since the number of Roman public baths was large, used *oil* for cleaning their bodies. Also mustard and egg yolk seem to have a remarkably strong cleansing effect on the human body.

a strange contrast to the Tibetan multitude, who entirely neglect their bodies.

From time to time these ascetics fast during considerable periods, but why do these people fast ? Because they want to be spiritual, happy and healthy, and because they expect that they will be able greatly to prolong their lives by taking good care of their bodies.

I had to think of a Western health apostle whom I happen to know. He is about sixty years of age now and has taken the greatest care of his kidneys for forty years by carefully avoiding food which would not be good for them. He now has a serious kidney disease which seems to have been brought about by his continual fear for his kidneys.

Surely spirituality cannot be attained by physical practices. On the other hand, it is just as foolish to neglect one's body. I thought that these *gnen-dnas* ascetics badly needed a good dose of common sense.

CHAPTER IV

THE UNDERGROUND CITY OF THE INITIATES

I KNEW from Narbu that the City of the Initiates was an important centre situated in the Valley of Mystery at a distance of about twenty miles from the nearest village. I wondered again and again how a whole city could keep unwelcome visitors and the curious multitude away, all the more so as Narbu had told me that the City was not surrounded by walls or ditches and that it was not even guarded, an ordinary Tibetan monastery being infinitely better protected than the City.

In one of the smaller side valleys of the Sangpo Valley I could not get over the temptation of casually asking a young Tibetan farmer whether he had ever heard of the Valley of Mystery. He looked at me in a very strange way and replied, "*Me, me!*"* But there was something in his whole attitude that made it seem probable for the attentive observer that he did know something about it but was reluctant to talk. The Valley of Mystery was less than three days' walk distant and if there really was a city inhabited by many hundreds of people it was improbable that he had never heard of its existence.

"Surely the Valley of Mystery must exist," I insisted, "for I am going to it."

_____
* "No !"

He gave a start and then observed, almost tremblingly, in a very low voice :

"Of course, most of us know that the City exists, but it is an unwritten law that none of us should ever speak about it, or even mention its name."

"I know the way," I said, once more examining Narbu's sketch drawn with the accuracy of an officer on a Western General Staff. "I do not want to make you talk as I shall soon find out all about it myself. Tell me only *why* you are not allowed to talk and who forces so many thousands of people to hold their tongues."

"Dreadful punishment comes automatically to all those who break this rule," he answered. "We know this by experience. Last year two friends of mine passed on some rumours they had heard about the City. They were both taken very ill the same evening, and all their cattle died. The same and even worse things happen to all those who try to get near the City out of curiosity."

"Did you ever try it ?" I asked.

"No," he replied, "and this is the last question I can answer. I never went there, but a friend of mine tried it. He had passed the borderline marking the precincts of the City and returned some time later to join his friends who had accompanied him. He looked three years older and had become mute. He could not speak for three months. His *tshe** was paralysed."

I went on my way.

—————————

* Tongue.

I was not inclined to take the story very seriously, although the peasant had seemed greatly frightened. Once such fears get a firm hold of a whole population auto-suggestion becomes a mighty factor. Why should a powerful degree of auto-suggestion not bring about disease and paralysis? I had found cases of this kind in other parts of the world.

Two days later I approached the City of the Initiates.

I was in the valley indicated in Narbu's sketch.

At a place where it was about a hundred yards wide the river bed suddenly disappeared. Here stood a few large stone slabs displaying the word "Border" chiselled into the stone in large characters. So this was the "borderline"* the Tibetan peasant had mentioned to me!

I passed on. The valley beyond the stone slabs looked exactly like the area on the other side of it, with the difference that the river bed had suddenly disappeared. I walked several hundred yards farther, but no city came in view. A few hundred yards farther on the valley gradually widened, but still no city was visible. I began to wonder whether I had lost my way.

When I had walked a few more minutes I suddenly noticed a circular stone wall measuring about four feet in height and about ten yards in diameter, erected in the middle of the valley where it was about 400 yards wide. The ground very gently sloped from that circular wall in all directions, and in a much wider circle—the radius of

---
* Tsam.

which was perhaps 100 yards—there were seven
quadrangular railings.

I approached. The nearer I came the more I
could see how tidy and remarkably well kept everything seemed to be.

Then I noticed that the seven railings enclosed
seven quadrangular patches of ground entirely

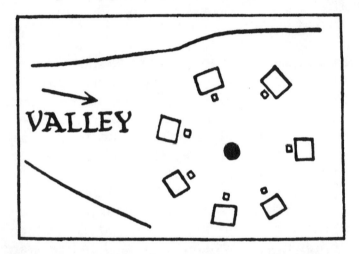

covered with large slabs made of glass. The area
of each quadrangle was about forty by forty yards.

In front of each quadrangle a staircase led underground to a substantial door. It was obvious that
the seven quadrangles were so many residential
buildings built into the ground, the light coming
in through flat glass ceilings on a level with the
ground. I at once realized the idea of the designer
of these strange "houses". It would be easy to
keep them warm in the winter. At the same time
the City would be practically earthquake-proof, and
as the "roofs" were on a level with the ground it

would be sufficient to cover the glass surfaces with sand and to remove the railings and the little wall in the centre to make the whole City disappear in cases of emergency. In the worst event even the staircases could be covered up.

The light of the morning sun made the glass surfaces glitter, and I began to wonder how the inhabitants protected themselves from the scorching rays of the sun in the hot summer afternoons, when I noticed a large pipe leading up to a kind of tank in the circular wall in the centre, which was situated at the highest point of the gently sloping plain. Smaller pipes ran out from the tank towards the glass surfaces, and it was probable that on hot afternoons the temperature of the houses could be kept down by a continual flow of water over the glass roofs.

I went down one of the staircases and stood before a heavy door. There was no device at all by which a visitor could signal his presence. I knocked with my fingers and a little later with my fist. But no one came to open. I had the idea to get on the glass roofs and trample in order to wake somebody, but found that this was quite impossible as the railings were more than eight feet high, very substantial, and so ingeniously devised that climbing over them was impossible.

So all I could do was to stroll about, looking for someone. But nobody was abroad. I seemed to be in a City of the Dead. And yet it was perhaps half past nine in the morning!

I decided to take a little walk to examine the neighbourhood, hoping to meet someone on my return. I walked out of the City in the opposite direction, but once I was beyond the railings of the last glass surface I was again in the desert, and a quarter of a mile farther on there were other stone slabs again displaying the word "Border". That was all!

So I turned round to walk back. The City of the Initiates lay before me at a distance of a few hundred yards, but had I come there for the first time unaware of its existence I should not have noticed it. The thin railings, which were exactly the same colour as the ground, were hardly visible and the circular wall was hidden by a little ridge.

When I had returned I saw somebody come up one of the seven staircases. It was not necessary to call him. He came along to meet me with great rapidity.

"*Chi la iru dug?*"* he asked sharply.

He wore a *chu-pa* made of cheap silk and was scrupulously clean. His eyes were very cold. There did not seem to be any expression in his face.

"I have been invited to come here," I answered.

"By whom?" His voice sounded almost hollow, and was impersonal in tone.

I mentioned Narbu's name.

His cold aloofness at once gave way to great respect.

"It is too early, sir; very few people in the City get up before noon. Life here begins in the early afternoon. If you have been invited to come here, Lha-mo-chun† will know about it. You must wait. Perhaps she will come out from the palace in an hour."

---

* "What do you want here?"   † The little goddess.

"The palace !" I exclaimed.

"Yes, the palace," he repeated. "That is the palace." He pointed to one of the quadrangular glass surfaces.

He bowed respectfully and passed on.

During the whole conversation his eyes had remained quite aloof.

I looked at him while he walked away. Another man dressed in cotton came up from another staircase. I did not like his gait at all. I could not help thinking of the doll in a well-known operetta by Offenbach. There was no life about this man, not a shade of individuality. The coldest valet having lived for years with the coldest aristocrat in the world would be a volcano of life and feeling in comparison with this man. When he passed me I got a glimpse of his eyes. They were almost glassy, like the eyes of a corpse.

To use my time I once more examined everything very carefully. I had not yet explored the wall and leaned over it. It was built round a vertical shaft. I looked down. It seemed to be enormously deep. I strained my eyes. Down it went, and seemed to disappear in the bowels of the earth. I looked for a stone. If I threw down a good-sized stone about ten pounds in weight I could ascertain its depth, I thought. The City was so tidy that not a single stone covered the ground. I had to walk at least five minutes to fetch a few good-sized stones.

I threw one of them down into the shaft and listened. Ten seconds passed and there was no sound. Twenty, thirty, forty, fifty seconds passed and yet no sound came ! I threw down a second heavy stone and leaned over the wall. There was no sound at all !

I walked towards the mountain-side a second time and fetched a big stone weighing at least twenty pounds. I pulled out my rubber boat from the bag made of sheepskin in which it was hidden and with the help of strings and safety-pins turned it into a large earphone, fastening it to the wall of the shaft, the wide opening turned downward.

I then threw down the heavy stone and listened through the earphone with the greatest attention. Ten seconds passed, then twenty, then thirty ! No sound yet ! I was in the greatest suspense. After about thirty-five seconds I heard the sound of the heavy stone as it savagely tore along the wall of the shaft. The brushing against the wall continued for several seconds, but by the fortieth second it had not yet struck the bottom. I listened through my earphone for another minute but did not hear the faintest sound.

Surely this was an interesting object of study for any explorer, and I walked once more to the mountain-side and returned with a piece of rock weighing a little over thirty pounds.

At that moment another Tibetan ran up to me from one of the staircases, saying :

"My lord, our guest, you are respectfully requested not to throw stones into the shaft."

He looked at me icily with his glassy eyes and walked away.

Soon afterwards the City seemed to awaken to life. People came up the various staircases, most of them humbly dressed in cotton gowns. A few others were dressed in silk. The inhabitants seemed to belong to two different categories. Those dressed in silk moved about like human beings. When some of them passed me while I stood leaning against the wall of the shaft they greeted me without, however, stopping or putting any questions. Their faces were rather handsome in most cases, and a few women were very beautiful. Only their eyes had a kind of dismal expression. None of them laughed, and those who talked to each other while they passed from one "building" to another spoke in an exceedingly low voice.

The people wearing cotton *chu-pas* were quite different. They were more numerous than the other variety and seemed to be the servants of the colony. There were even children belonging to that category. This class of people was rather horrible to look at. They behaved like automatons and their eyes strangely resembled the eyes of corpses.

I began to feel a little uncomfortable. But then I thought of beautiful little Dolma so full of life and enthusiasm, and of Narbu, who was so clever, energetic, and kind-hearted. Could such people introduce me to a Body not serving the purpose of Light? Had I not been told that the City of the Initiates took a stand for the most lofty principles? Did it not work to help the world?

And then everything about the City seemed to be so tidy, so practical, so remarkably well organized. The very plan of the City bore the unmistakable stamp of genius.

A few children dressed in cotton garbs passed

the wall, carrying heavy packages.   A little girl
dropped a parcel just while she passed me.   I
stooped to help her to pick it up.   Our eyes met.   I
had never seen such eyes in a child.   There was no
life in them, no joy, no enthusiasm, only the
monotonous expression of a mechanically working
intelligence.   She took the parcel without saying a
word or smiling, and passed on.*   Again I had to
think of a robot or a wandering corpse.

At that moment one of the adult automatons,
dressed in a *chu-pa*,† approached me, gazed at me
lifelessly and said :

"My lord, our guest, Lha-mo-chun‡ will meet
you at the entrance of the palace."

I walked to one of the staircases directed by the
lifeless servant.   A young lady, elegantly dressed in
pure white silk of excellent quality, ascended the
staircase and met me smilingly.

"Welcome !" she said in a very low voice.   "We
knew that you were coming."

"I arrived here this morning," I replied in Tibetan, "but had not the pleasure to meet anybody at
first."

"We rise very late in the Holy City," she replied.
"Breakfast is served in the dining-house"—she
pointed to one of the other glass roofs—"at one
o'clock.   All our members and guests are present
then."   She glanced at my equipment.   "I shall
have these things transported to your room."   She
beckoned to one of the servants dressed in cotton

---

* Only once I met two children in the City who seemed to be really
alive.   They were probably children of members.
† Tibetan gown.   ‡ The little goddess.

chu-pas, who got hold of my belongings. "You will live in the guest-house over there."

The servant walked away with my things.

"You are the second white person who visits the Holy City," she said ; and then she added in broken English : "There have been several people here from India, but only one from the West."

"Has he returned ?" I asked, this time in English.

"No," she answered. "Unfortunately, he died here. He is buried in the Holy City."

"Would it be too much to ask you to have someone show me his grave tomorrow ?" I hazarded.

"By no means," she went on in fairly comprehensible English. "I will show it to you myself."

We walked a few dozen yards to the next staircase.

"This is the temple-building," she said. "We call it *Lha-Khang*." She pulled out a golden key and unlocked the door.

"Please, my lord, step in first."

Decidedly they were very polite in the Holy City.

We entered a corridor. The light was almost too strong for one's eyes, the whole roof being made of glass, and brilliant daylight flooding in through the whole ceiling. She unlocked the heavy door opposite and threw it open. The walls were covered with strange magic signs and *dsungs*.*

"This is the dead-house," she said. "When someone dies in the Holy City, his or her remains are kept here until burial."

"For how long ?"

---

* Magic formulae.

"For seven days," answered Lha-mo-chun. "There are three floors in this building," she went on. "The dead-house is on the top floor, our temple is on the floor just below it, and the burial-place is on the floor under the temple."

We walked out and she carefully locked the door.

On going downstairs we passed the door of the temple, which seemed to consist of massive gold. Perhaps the layer of gold was superficial, but even in that case the illusion was complete.

"I am sorry I cannot show you the temple," she said. "Only the members of the Holy Brotherhood are allowed to enter. For guests special permission of Him, our Prince, is required, but He is not in the City at present."

We went downstairs to the lowest floor. The light in the corridor was very dim as it came successively through three glass ceilings. She again pulled out a golden key and unlocked a large hall. "This is our cemetery," she said. "You will find the grave of the Westerner in the corner over there. It is the second from the right."

I walked up to the stone slab. A Tibetan name was written on it. I read it very carefully but found that it did not sound Western at all. He was probably buried under the Tibetan name by which he had been known in the City.

I was lingering before a few other stone slabs when she said :

"If you like I will show you rapidly the other buildings. As He is absent, I can even show you His private garden. If we hurry up a little I can show you all the buildings in the Holy City except, of course, His palace. I hope He will grant you an audience when He returns and then you may see this too."

We went upstairs, and she took me to the building situated on the other side of the palace.

When she opened the heavy door I could hardly believe my eyes. There was a large hall measuring about forty by forty yards full of delicious flowers. The glasshouse was just as good as any of the best to be found in botanical gardens in the West. The hall was divided into various compartments, kept at different temperatures by hot-water pipes.

The greenhouse was nothing exceptional in itself, but it seemed to be almost a miracle to find such a thing in a Tibetan valley.

"This is His private garden," she said with the deepest respect. "This is where He, our Prince, Mani Rimpotche, the exalted Jewel or Prince of Light, deigns to take his afternoon walks. The glasshouse is directly connected with the palace by a subterranean passage."

We had entered a compartment where tropical plants were kept.

"May I ask you what kind of fuel you use in the Holy City in your central-heating system?"

"We use alcohol," she answered. "It burns smokelessly."

"From where do you get it?"

"We distil it ourselves. The distillery is in the building just opposite. The building is used for distilling, cooking, washing linen, centres of sanitation, and as a residential building for several hundred servants."

We left the glasshouse.

"The building over there is the residential house of our members," she said. "You will live in the guest-house, opposite. You can come and go as you like. You will see the dining-building very soon, when we take breakfast. I will now show you rapidly the building used for cooking and sanitation."

We walked over to the other "building" and went downstairs. A heavy door stood wide open. There was a large announcement which proclaimed that members, guests, and servants had to use the sanitary conveniences in that building, which was connected for that purpose with the other buildings by subterranean passages.

"Would it not be more practical to instal sanitary conveniences in each of the other buildings?" I ventured to ask the superintendent of the building, a middle-aged man wearing a cheap silk robe.

"No," he said. "There are occult reasons for this strict rule. All impure organic matter here instantly goes into a fire kept burning day and night. Everybody in the Holy City must go to the inconvenience of walking a few hundred yards from his or her building to this one. This is a sacrifice brought to the purity of the Holy City."

In saying so, his tone denoted considerable contempt for "impure organic matter". I could not help thinking that respect of the Creator automatically implied a deep respect for our own bodies, and that the contempt of physical needs was nothing short of a sin. Up to that time I had maintained a very critical and matter-of-fact attitude about everything I saw or heard in the City of the Initiates.

Strange to say, after taking my first meal in the dining-building I stopped viewing things in this manner and suddenly became enthusiastic about everything in the Holy City as if I had swallowed with the food a strange capacity for uncritical enthusiasm.

Several hundred members and guests of the Holy Brotherhood were present in the dining-building to take breakfast. The meal was served in a large hall measuring about forty by forty yards. There were many elevated platforms,* the participants being seated on them in circles of nine people each,† each person sitting on an expensive cushion of the very highest quality. Dozens of those dreadful lifeless servants—whom I greatly disliked until I had taken my first meal in the Holy City—moved about noiselessly on thick carpets. The food was sent over from the kitchen and sanitation-building through an underground passage. Everything seemed to be very well organized. Servants came and went at regular intervals and one of them even seemed to regulate the traffic.

---

* Some of my readers will have wondered how the Brotherhood obtain the means of living. If only a few dozen out of the several hundred members of the Fraternity were about as wealthy as Narbu, all expenses could be met out of their voluntary contributions, all the more so as it is highly probable that the servants of the Colony receive no wages at all. Furthermore, the perfect organization of the Holy City tends to reduce expenses by rendering waste impossible. As to the food supplies to the City, only a portion of the actual needs of the Brotherhood seemed to have been purchased from the outside world. There were vast underground halls covered with glass which were not accessible, and these may have been used for growing some food on scientific lines.

† The number nine seemed to be the "holy number" in the Holy City, although seven also frequently occurred. There were seven buildings; the guest-house had ninety guest-rooms. The gong was sounded nine times before meals, etc.

A few of the members could speak broken English about as much as Lha-mo-chun, and two of them happened to sit in my circle. When I saw the servant regulating the traffic at the entrance to the passage leading to the kitchen-building, I cracked a joke about the City having an equivalent of traffic constables in the West, and accompanied the jest by a laugh.

The others looked greatly shocked. I was at once politely but very firmly informed by a kind of super-intendent dressed in cheap silk that laughter was forbidden in the Holy City.

I then learned from the other members in my circle that not only laughter but also speaking in a loud voice was a breach of the rules. Only conversation in a low voice was tolerated.

Among the people seated in my circle many were clairvoyants. They were very proud of their occult achievements. They also felt proud that they had been selected by Mani Rimpotche, the Exalted Jewel, to serve Him in the great mission of bringing illumination to the world.

The exact hierarchical order of the members of the Holy Brotherhood headed by the Prince of Light or Exalted Jewel, occasionally briefly referred to as "Him", was a secret. The members passed through successive initiations, each initiation raising them to a higher degree in the Hierarchy of Light. Amongst the lofty titles I heard while I stayed in the Valley of Mystery there were such as Dispensers of the Divine Wisdom, Masters of Light, Disciples of Light, Saviours of Souls, Lords of Compassion, Illuminated Teachers, and so forth. Each initiation tied the holder of the title more closely to the head of the Brotherhood, and I think the holders of the highest degrees had no separate personality left at all and were mere "agents of the Divine will", heart, body and soul.

In return for their pledging themselves to the "Light" they obtained greater occult powers and spiritual energies on the understanding that all of them would be used only in the interest of the Brotherhood and for no other purpose.

Any thought of sex in the Holy City seemed to be regarded as contemptible and beneath the dignity of such highly spiritual people.

I looked around and saw Lha-mo-chun seated in one of the other circles at a distance of about ten yards. No one seemed to be aware of the very existence of "sex" in the Holy City when looking at a man or a woman, no matter how handsome or beautiful he or she happened to be.

After breakfast I had to comply with the only formality compulsory to guests visiting the Holy City. On entering the guest-house I had to hand over to the superintendent a small piece of paper on which I had written a few words in Tibetan letters.

I entered my room. It was fairly large and splendidly lit by the enormous "window" covering the whole ceiling. It was early in the hot summer afternoon, but nevertheless the room remained cool owing to the automatic device mentioned before by which varying amounts of water could be poured out over the glass roofs to regulate the temperature. Ventilation was effected by a system of pipes probably leading to a kind of fan serving the whole building and kept going continually by the servants.*

As the superintendent knew that I was a white person they had put in a Western bed. The door of the room could be bolted from the inside and everything was scrupulously clean. The superintendent had told me that I could do everything in my room except eating and washing my linen. The rooms must not be "desecrated" by eating, he said, and the washing of clothes, etc., was to be done by the servants in the sanitation-building.

Everything seemed to be all right as far as physical comfort was concerned except the prospect of having to walk again and again many hundred yards to go to the sanitation-building, and being a man of a free and independent disposition I at once decided to simplify matters in this respect by setting aside the largest of my bottles for a convenient purpose denied to me by the strict rules of the house. The whole psychical atmosphere of the City seemed to be very strange and had a tendency to develop latent powers in man.

When I left the guest-building in the morning the outer door was sometimes closed, but on other occasions it stood wide open. Strange to say, I always *felt* before I left my room whether the outer door was open or closed, and this vague feeling

---

* When passing the door of the "house" I had noticed that it was quite an exceptional entrance for a Tibetan building. It looked absolutely air- and water-tight. Moreover, when I entered my room I found that there was no possibility of opening any of the glass slabs of which the ceiling consisted, ventilation being effected through a system of air pipes. Did all this indicate that the Underground City had been built with a view to the possibility of flooding it in case of emergency?

(it was *not* what is known as clairvoyance) proved to be correct on all occasions, for when I reached the outer door after passing through two different corridors situated at right angles I always found that the outer door stood open, half open, or was closed, just as I had sensed it in my room. The phenomenon was inexplicable but it was a fact, subjectively.*

A second very strange experience I had the same day when I walked over to the sanitation-building to pour out the contents of the bottle I had provided in my room for a convenient purpose. I found that the liquid had turned black! At the moment I attributed the fact to the food, and a few minutes later I had forgotten all about it.

The psychical atmosphere of the City seemed to render critical and methodical thinking very difficult. It tended to weaken memory (I had been in the City for less than ten hours and felt as if these hours had been so many years), but it seemed to develop the intuitional nature of man to a remarkable degree.

When I had returned to my room I heard the noise of numerous footsteps on the glass roof. One could hear the rumble of thunder in the distance, and as the Tibetan thunderstorms are usually very violent in the summer and are often accompanied by hailstones, a kind of thick cloth or thin mattress was put on the glass roofs to protect them from

---

* The members of the Secret Society could not leave the City unless sent out on special missions assigned to them by the Ruler. Their life seemed to be regulated like that of the inhabitants of an anthill. And as to the servants, they seemed to be so devoid of life and supra-animal intelligence that it seemed to be *impossible* for them to do anything except their duties.

the hail. I went upstairs to watch these proceedings and found that the surface of the buildings was teeming with perhaps a hundred of those lifeless servants, who were assisted by a large number of mechanically moving children whose lifeless glaze reminding one of a corpse was perhaps even more unpleasant than the expression—or rather lack of any expression—in the eyes of the servants.

The room was darkened by the mattresses put on the glass roofs and, after having lit a lamp, I sat down to study (they had specially provided for me a kind of case to serve the purpose of a Western table and a Western chair). Half an hour later nine loud strokes of a gong were heard, and as I had not risen within twenty seconds to leave the room to go to the dining-building, a lifeless servant came in without knocking and said :

"My lord, our guest, will you please go to the second meal of the day ?"

In the dining-hall I met Narbu, who had just arrived from his *dsong*. He looked very fit. Only the expression of his eyes seemed to have altered a little. They were still beautiful, but had just a slight touch of a glassy appearance which I did not like at all. He seemed to occupy a very high rank in the Occult Hierarchy, as the other members seemed to approach him with unusual marks of respect.

Narbu informed me that Mani Rimpotche, the Exalted Jewel or Prince of Light, the Ruler of the Holy City, was expected to return the following day and that it was quite possible that I would be granted the privilege of an audience. There were cases, he added, where acquaintances of certain members of the Holy Brotherhood had sacrificed their whole fortune and travelled a thousand miles to obtain an audience of Him lasting only two minutes. If he succeeded in arranging the audience with the Exalted Jewel I might ask the Prince of Light for permission to attend divine service. Only members were allowed to enter the temple, and guests who had not yet pledged themselves to anything required a special permit for doing so which could only be granted by the Exalted Prince of Light Himself.

The next few days would be of vital importance for me, said Narbu. No one here had a right to force my hand and I had to decide quite freely whether I wanted to become a member. I was quite free to come and go as I liked, and so long as I had not taken a pledge I was under no obligation to the Holy Brotherhood. Then he whispered: "Many of us here realize of what enormous value you could be to us if you decided to join us of your own free will." He even hinted at a quick rise in the ranks of the Hierarchy, rapidly succeeding initiations and the possibility of my being entrusted with a "really big job" once I had decided to become a member.

I pointed out that I had never joined any association or fraternity of any kind, and that up to the present I had at all times made an effort to maintain absolute independence in every respect, and that I felt considerable reluctance to relinquish that attitude.

"It is you who will have to decide," he said, "and

the moment you have taken your decision the Prince of Light will assign to you the exalted position in which you will be most useful."

I thought that I had always assigned myself my own position and that I had acquired knowledge and priceless experience by doing so, but I could not examine things in the City quite as intelligently as I could have done in a really neutral atmosphere. I felt as if my capacity to think deeply and freely and to weigh matters coolly was impaired by my very presence in it. And as I am a man of what occultists call the "lion temperament", although very meek when I *want* to be meek, everything in me revolted. I then almost cursed the atmosphere of that city.

I had to think of a passage in the drama *Faust*, by Goethe, where the devil says to himself after leaving a prospective victim :

> "Contempt your capacity to think,
> Which is man's greatest power ;
> Welcome misty things and sorcery
> And the spirit of illusion,
> Then I shall get you surely enough."

Then I again looked at Narbu and felt ashamed to have entertained such thoughts. He seemed to feel so sincere about it. He wanted me to join a Brotherhood working for the good of the world, and gave me freedom to make my choice. The pendulum swung back once more and I felt a perfect beast to have entertained these thoughts.

There was lively conversation in our circle, although everybody seemed to take pains not to raise his voice.

THE UNDERGROUND CITY 117

All these people were a little proud to have the privilege of working for the world. They had a rather high opinion of their own spirituality. Some of them even linked up the Prince of Light with certain highly placed spiritual entities who are what Hindu philosophers call karmic agents and regulate the unloading of karmic reactions on men and nations. Some of them even seemed to feel that the Holy Ruler could actually influence the destinies of the world by hastening or retarding the outbreak of wars, the evolution of new types of epidemics and the disappearance of older kinds of disease, as well as the action of other scourges of humanity, including the various catastrophes of Nature. They seemed to consider the Holy Jewel as a kind of supreme judge dispensing Divine justice, and naturally felt very elated at the thought of standing so near a being who possessed all these powers.

Human intelligence they only held in mediocre esteem. They seemed to feel that man's mission was to get past the human stage, and that passing beyond the limited matter-of-fact intelligence of man and soaring to intuitive levels was the best method of becoming more "Divine".

Again the pendulum of my disposition towards the City swayed in the opposite direction. I thought of the devil speaking in Goethe's *Faust* (the verses cited above), but it was enough for me to look once more at Narbu to make the pendulum swing back again. The longer I stayed in the Holy City the more I seemed to be overcome by a frightful state of indecision and experienced the most acute sense of spiritual anguish. At times I felt as if the ground disappeared under my feet, that everything was in a state of flux, and as if I were tossed about by conflicting spiritual currents.

I listened to Narbu while he took part in the conversation. I felt as if his voice had become still more metallic and hollow.   When I made a few casual remarks I began to pay attention to my own voice, and found, to my astonishment, that it sounded unusually hollow too. The fine individual touch which a man's personality gives to his voice* seemed to be absent.

I listened to the conversation of the people seated in the neighbouring circle. They were talking on evolution.

People in the City did not seem to talk much about any human topics.   All of them seemed to want to get past the human stage and to be God-like.

One of them envisaged the glory of evolution, life passing from the mineral stage through plants, animals, man and angels up to the archangelic and Divine stages, every creature automatically becoming a god.   And one day it *would* be Godlike.   It was only a question of time.

Glory, in their eyes, seemed to be the automatic and inevitable destiny of man. They did not seem to be aware of the dreadful alternative of annihilation, of the fact

---

* Especially people who have gone through great soul-passion, this greatest gift of God, as it welds us more and more into one unit with our soul, have a fine human touch in their voices.   I imagine Shakespeare, the real Shakespeare who sketched all those wonderful characters having souls of their own, must have had this beautiful "timbre" in his voice, making one think of an Angel of the Creator.

that there is a downward trend of satanic evolution as a counterpart to the upward trend of Divine evolution.

They seemed to feel that the great spiritual struggle was *between spirit and matter.* They seemed to utterly ignore the vital fact that there are two different types of spirituality, the upward trend and the lower one, and that *the real spiritual struggle is one between two different types of spirituality with matter serving as the battleground.*

The food of the second meal of the day consisted of nine different dishes served in fairly rapid succession so that the second meal of the day (only two meals were taken per day) should not last longer than about an hour. The food was served on silver plates of very original design. It tasted very nice, but it was very difficult to know exactly of what it consisted. It obviously contained some meat, a fact I immediately noticed because I happen to eat meat only occasionally. Most of the food was a kind of ragout. The nine dishes served varied in taste, but the contents of each plate were one uniform mass of food.

The quantities served were small. The contents of all the nine plates put together hardly equalled in quantity about half the amount of food eaten by an average Londoner for dinner. The food was strangely nourishing and satisfying. All the substances which might have caused flatulence seemed to have been eliminated with the greatest care.

Narbu invited me to join a few other members of the Holy Brotherhood after dinner, but I thanked him and went to bed soon after eight o'clock. I understood that the life of the Holy City only reached its culminating point late in the evening, most of the members and guests going to bed between one and two o'clock in the morning.

I had a dreadfully restless night, perhaps the worst I had had for years. I tossed wildly about, shaken by terrible dreams. Sometimes when I was half-way between waking and dreaming I felt as though the room was filled with demons in white clothes with a slight reddish touch, trying to tear my heart open and take something out of it with their horrible claws. My whole body writhed with pain and I was bathed in perspiration. Two or three light figures, who were somewhat like the other demons, stood near me. They looked like boys of about sixteen, and their eyes flashed like so many sheets of lightning every time the demons made a dash for my heart, and thus drove them back again and again.

The nightmare increased in intensity. My whole body shivered. I passed through the stages of half slumber, deep sleep, and full consciousness with incredible rapidity. When fully conscious I thought I had caught some serious infectious disease causing high fever.

A few seconds later I was again in a semi-conscious condition. Hundreds of white angels with a slight reddish touch on their bright garments and having beautiful but dismal eyes—all of them having almost the same face—advanced threateningly, their white claws all aimed at my heart as if they were determined to snatch something hidden in it. When this dreadful army approached once more, the boys dressed in white advanced to protect me. Their faces had an individual touch, each boy having a facial expression entirely different from the other. Their eyes flashed and sheets of lightning came out from them directed at those demons dressed in beautiful and resplendent reddish-white robes. But the flashes of lightning were too weak to hold the whole army of demons at bay. The boys recoiled. For the first time an indescribable expression of anxiety came into their handsome faces.

I awoke to full consciousness. My whole body was writhing. I had high fever. My lips were parched and my tongue dry. I knew enough of medicine to realize that my blood approached coagulation point and that if the fever increased by only another degree I should die. I tossed about in bed, too weak to call anyone, and there was no bell.

After a second's full consciousness I lapsed back into my former condition.

The boys in pure white robes still looked very concerned. All their feelings found a visible impression in their expressive faces. They stood behind me, but during my nightmare I could see forward and backward at the same time. The demons, however, had no individual expression in their faces. They were all alike. There was no personality about them. They seemed to mechanically carry out the behests of someone else.

The boys seemed to possess strong individualities. This very individuality was their best defence against the large army of spiritual dummies. But it grew too hot for them. Another few seconds and they would be vanquished and my heart torn open by the demons.

Then one of the boys blew a silver trumpet, and, with the suddenness of an eagle pouncing down from the sky, a glorious figure descended from Heaven like a flash of lightning. His face was a curious mixture of the face of a lion and that of a handsome young man. His voice sounded like the roar of the sea swelling into one mighty harmony when he almost roared the words, "Leave this child alone !" and struck the host of demons with a sword that seemed to be made of solar substance, as it shone like the sun in all its glory.

The demons scattered in all directions. Some of them fled, others suddenly turned into mice, rats, and frogs, and disappeared in the ground, and all was quiet.

I was fully conscious again. I felt that the fever had just reached its highest point, and that I was on the mend. For the first time in many years I had been actually ill. I was too weak to stand up to fetch something to wipe away the perspiration in which I was bathed. Only half an hour later I felt strong enough to stand up and light the lamp.

I had no further nightmares that night. I only felt terribly thirsty and drank several pints of water.

In the forenoon, while everybody else in the Holy City seemed to be asleep, I went out for a walk. I had never walked so slowly since I had entered Tibet. When I was a mile outside the City of the Initiates I stripped off my clothes and took a sun-bath in the glorious sunshine.

I took in the flood of warmth and life with great gratitude. Never before had I felt such an influx of strength in such a short time.

About noon I walked back. After coming home I drank a few more pints of water, and when the gong sounded nine times to mark breakfast-time I had almost entirely recovered. When I smilingly greeted Narbu he only observed that I looked a little thinner. He had not the faintest idea that I had been within inches of death the night before.

Just as we sat down to breakfast a message was handed to Narbu on a golden plate. He reverently broke the seal. He could hardly hide his emotion when he told me :

"Mani Rimpotche, the Exalted Jewel, arrived here unexpectedly yesterday at midnight. I had an audience of the Prince of Light at two o'clock this morning and mentioned you to him."

"Did he know something about me ?"

"I think he did. But all he was graciously pleased to say was that I should at once give instructions to all concerned that you should be treated with quite exceptional courtesy and attention, and that the matter of your audience which I had respectfully proposed to him would be examined a little later.

"And now," added Narbu, "I have just received his decision. You will be received at the palace at three o'clock tomorrow afternoon, and I notice that a full half-hour has been set aside for your audience, which I can assure you is an exceptionally long time. Even so-called long audiences granted by the Prince of Light do not last longer than seven minutes, and only once in years has so great a privilege been accorded to a guest coming to the City of the Initiates. I hope you like the city," added Narbu.

"Yes," I observed politely; "everything here seems to be so very clean and so well organized."

"And how about the psychical atmosphere? Are you pleased with that?"

"It is very strange," I said. "I feel like someone who is dead and has forgotten to leave behind his physical body."

"You mean you feel like a man who visits the Beyond in the flesh?"

"Yes," I said. "It is a very strange feeling and a very strange place."

"The culminating point of your stay will be your audience with Him," Narbu observed.

Breakfast, which consisted of only one somewhat more substantial dish, was over, and I walked back to my room. I first took several hours' rest to recover as much as possible of my strength lost in the fever, and then began to wash a piece of linen. I was fully aware of the fact that I broke another rule of the city by washing my linen in the room instead of giving it to a servant to be handled in the sanitation-building; but as I am always reluctant to let other people touch my own personal effects and never use other people's services when it is not absolutely necessary, I bolted the door and began to wash that piece myself.

Hardly had I soaked the linen when the wooden bowl which stood in the room for washing suddenly broke into several small pieces. It was a most unusual experience. The bowl was fairly strong and I had handled it with the usual care.

Later in the afternoon I met some of Narbu's friends whose acquaintance I had made in the dining-building.   I still felt a little tired and did not talk very much myself, but their conversation, during which they discussed various internal affairs of the Holy City, proved to be extremely interesting.

I gathered, for instance, that sexual intercourse, even in the case of married people, could only be used for the purpose of procreation.   All sexual energy unused for this purpose had to be transformed into "higher" forces to serve the interests of the Brotherhood.   Even the sex force of the members does not belong to them but to the Prince. It must be used for begetting children to be brought up in his spirit or for the purpose of creating spiritual energy to fill the spiritual "reservoir" of the Initiates.   A veritable anthill mentality seemed to reign in the Holy City in regard to everything connected with sex matters.

I thought of my strange experience with the wooden bowl.   The Holy Brotherhood may have had ways and means of controlling even the most intimate marital secrets of their members !

Has life any meaning, I pondered, if we deprive it of all possibility of self-expression ?   What is life minus freedom, variety, and personality ?   A meaningless void !   In the house of the Creator there must be many abodes, I thought.   I had always believed that if I love and honour God, love my neighbour and love myself, God would let me do everything I like so long as I respected these three laws.

Conversation drifted to other topics.   Some of the members present expressed spiritual indignation at the many sins committed in the world.   They hoped that the Exalted Jewel would punish all those who caused so much injustice and so much suffering. I could not help feeling that practically all of the people present had a slight touch of what may be called spiritual arrogance. The most arrogant ones seemed to be the most sheepish ones when the conversation centred around the Prince of Light and the Great Holy Teachers.*

Late in the afternoon I returned to my room. The servant had replaced the broken bowl by another one and no one said a word about the matter. I tried to think clearly, but the longer I stayed in the Holy City the more difficult it seemed to be to keep out unconscious influences when forming one's thoughts.

I took dinner very quietly, smiled to Narbu, and returned to my room.

The faculty to think clearly diminished after each meal. Moreover, I felt that my body revolted against the food taken. I am a man of quick decisions. After the fourth meal taken in the Holy City it was obvious that the food did not agree with me. Moreover, every time I had eaten something in the dining-building I felt very strongly that unconscious influences impaired my capacity to think.

Maybe all this was mere coincidence or a wrong impression. Be that as it may, I decided not to take any chances.

I went to bed about 8 p.m. and had a much better night's rest than the day before. I awoke feeling

---

* Also amongst non-spiritual people the author has often noticed that arrogance and sheepishness go hand in hand.

much stronger and decided to walk and run twenty miles non-stop to the nearest village and back again to buy food.   I started at three in the morning and returned some time after twelve.

When the nine strokes of the gong sounded and the servant came in to announce in his dreadfully lifeless voice, "My lord our guest.   The first meal of the day is served," I simply said :

"I shall not go to breakfast."

He mechanically repeated his sentence :

"My lord our guest.   The first meal of the day is served."

I thought the fellow would make an excellent door-keeper and let him stand there to repeat his stereotyped phrase as often as he liked.

He then went to fetch the superintendent of the building.

I told the latter that I did not intend to partake of meals and did not wish to go to the dining-house.

"But, my lord, all our guests are expected to go to the dining-house twice a day."

"I shall not," I said, politely but firmly.   "I understood that guests here were free to do what they liked."

He bowed and withdrew.

Immediately afterwards a servant sent by Narbu came in inquiring whether I was ill.   I sent my greetings and the news that I was all right.

A minute later another servant sent by Lha-mo-chun arrived to gather information about my health.   I thanked her for her kind interest, adding the message that I was not ill and only required solitude instead of attention.

A little while later a third servant came along to learn whether my health permitted me to keep the time fixed for the audience in the palace in the afternoon. I replied that I should certainly come, and had I felt that I would be unable to come I should not have failed to let them know myself.

This brought the series of messages to a conclusion. I locked the door and calmly prepared my own breakfast, mixing barley-meal with a little butter and a few dried radishes. I had bought sufficient food in the village to last for at least four days.

Curiously enough, this self-prepared meal did not seem to impair my capacity to think, and I wondered whether this was an actual fact or a mere erroneous impression brought about by auto-suggestion.

An hour later I went to join Narbu and a few of his friends. I did not want this good and kind-hearted man to think that he or anyone else in the Holy City had done anything to offend me and to make him suspect that I had a discourteous reason for staying away from the meals.

Ten minutes before three I arrived at the palace for the audience.

At that moment I really thought the Prince of Light was a sincere spiritual leader and the head of an Occult Brotherhood whose supreme goal was to honour the Creator and help the world. The only thing I disliked about him was the extraordinary cloud of majesty with which he seemed to surround himself. But then I thought it might be a mere compromise. He probably felt that he could carry out his work much better if he cloaked himself with such an appearance. And as I am always inclined to look for the substance rather than the shadow, I did not consider this splendour to be a proof of insincerity. Most people do such things on a smaller scale, I thought. At the time when I gave my first broadcast in 1933 I positively detested collars, which I considered both unpractical and idiotic, and yet when I went to see the talks executive in a continental country I did put on a collar, because I realized that if I appeared in the broadcasting house minus a collar I should never succeed in securing an interview with the talks executive, and that it would be stupid to sacrifice the opportunity of giving a broadcast for the sake of not putting on a collar. The Prince of Light, I thought, was doing the same thing on a larger scale, and I was prepared to pardon him.

I walked down the palace stairs. The entrance was guarded. Four "lifeless" servants stood there like so many stone statues. A fifth servant approached, bowed, and lighted a torch. The heavy double door was swung open by other servants, and after a pause of about two minutes I was escorted downstairs by not less than seven servants. Down and down we went. Landing followed landing. I had never realized how enormous such an underground building could be. At least twelve landings were behind us when we arrived at the bottom of the staircase situated at a depth of perhaps a hundred feet under the main entrance of the palace. Another heavy door was swung open and I found myself in a small hall lit by torches. The time was exactly three o'clock. Obviously our paces had been timed very carefully so as to make me arrive downstairs at three o'clock sharp, which was the time fixed for the audience.

Another servant approached with a golden sprayer and poured on me an abundant supply of perfume. I had certainly not expected to be fumigated in this manner before entering the inner precincts of the palace. But perhaps the Prince had established this wise general rule for his own benefit in case a person having *genuine* Tibetan ideas about hygiene and cleanliness should happen to be invited as a guest by a member of the Holy Brotherhood and secure an audience.

While I was being fumigated in this manner, I looked round. Nine small underground passages ran out from the small hall in all directions. They probably connected the palace with the other parts of the Underground City. The idea struck me that at least one of the underground passages may have been connected with a place several miles distant to enable the Prince or any of his lieutenants to enter and leave the Holy City in a secret manner. A system of air-pipes justified the assumption that at least two of the underground passages measured several miles in length. Each of the passages was guarded by at least four servants, some of them probably used for despatching messages. Wherever the visitor looked, his eyes fell on the lifeless faces of those servants who reminded one of so many corpses just risen from their coffins.

The heavy door on the opposite side of the small hall was thrown open.

I entered the large entrance-hall to the inner part

of the palace. From now onwards I only met members of the Brotherhood. No servant, as Narbu told me later, is permitted to enter the inner palace.

The large hall measured about thirty by forty yards. It was illuminated by hundreds of torches stuck into golden sockets in the walls and round the pillars, and fed through pipes with a liquid burning with a smokeless flame. Like many other halls in the Holy City, it was connected by air-pipes with a large room in the sanitation-building, where several dozen servants kept the fans going from about 11 a.m. to 3 a.m. the following day.

I was met by seven members of the Holy Brotherhood in gorgeous robes.

A thick black robe of pure silk embroidered with a large number of *dsungs** was brought, together with seven silk cushions. Slowly and ceremoniously the seven cushions were heaped one on another, and then one of the gorgeously dressed Brothers stepped on them, unfolded the robe, and got ready to cloak me with it.

At that moment the Masters of Ceremony probably received the greatest shock of their lives.

I flatly refused to put on a ceremonial robe of any kind.

"If your master is as great as you affirm," I said, politely but firmly, "he must know himself whether I am great or small. I do not want any special dress to improve my appearance when appearing before him."

They were dumbfounded. As Narbu told me in

---

* Magical formulae.

the evening, I had also broken the rule of absolute silence which must reign in the large underground hall and in the whole left half of the palace which is used by the Prince.   No one is allowed to utter a word there unless it is in reply to a question or in reference to a command uttered by the Prince of Light.

Several other Masters of Ceremony of a still higher rank were summoned in a hurry.   I was surrounded by an ever-increasing crowd of dignitaries who in turn tried to convince me in respectful whispers of the absolute necessity of putting on the black silk gown before stepping into the august presence of the Ruler.

So much fuss about such a formality! It really was funny.

After about five minutes' continual whispering I thought it was useless to take up their time any longer and said with profound respect:

"I apologize for having broken your rules, but I thought I had come here for an informal audience and not on solemn official business. Will you please present my respects to Mani Rimpotche?"

I turned towards the exit and began to walk out. The crowd of Masters of Ceremony rushed after me.

"You cannot go now," they whispered in a faltering voice. "The audience already began the moment you entered the inner part of the palace. An interrupted audience!   Such a thing has never been heard of!"

"I notice that the whole reception is intended to be mere ceremony," I said coolly.   "I have not come to the City to *get something*, but in order to assist and co-operate of my own free will with sincere spiritual helpers. I have no time for ceremonies. I suggest that one of you puts on that black silk robe and goes through the show on my behalf. I shall not put it on. This is final."

I bowed and turned towards the exit. They had no power to hold me back.

At that moment a high Court official dressed in pure white silk came running down from the staircase leading to the upper parts of the palace and literally shouted :

"Please stop ! The Exalted Jewel will welcome you as you are."

Narbu told me in the evening that it was for the first time in its history that someone had shouted in the inner part of the palace.

I returned.

The seven Masters of Ceremony walked in front with seven torches, and the Brothers of higher rank, who had been called to the rescue later on account of this unusual happening, brought up the rear.

On the upper landing I was respectfully welcomed by another high official wearing a white silk robe. We entered a richly decorated hall situated on top of the former one. Other Court officials approached. They could hardly believe their eyes when they saw a person coming up for an audience dressed in ordinary clothes. They advanced to take my shoes off and replace them by a pair of felt shoes richly adorned with silver ornaments.

I told them very politely that I was unwilling to let go of my own shoes, but if they thought they were not clean enough I had no objection to having them cleaned !

For the first time since I had entered the palace I saw a faint smile.

There were two staircases in this second hall, the right one, as Narbu told me later, leading to the private apartments of the Court officials, and the left one to the ceremonial rooms where the audience was to be held. An enormously long corridor, very wide and measuring several hundred yards in length, ran out from one of the walls of the hall, and for the first time the idea occurred to me that the Underground City might be very much larger than it appeared to be, and that only members who had passed the highest initiations had access to the most secret parts.

When we had ascended the staircase we reached a still more gorgeously decorated hall, this time dimly lit by daylight coming down through the ceiling. Nine other Masters of Ceremony, led by the Court Marshal, all dressed in white robes richly embroidered with gold, led me upstairs once more in a solemn procession. I realized that I was right near the audience-room, as we must have reached the uppermost part of the palace, since brilliant daylight was flooding in through the ceiling.

I was met by two members of the Brotherhood, probably acting in the capacity of private secretaries to the Prince.

The high official and the nine Masters of Ceremony dressed in white silk bowed and withdrew. I began to talk to the secretaries in a low voice, but they did not answer and put their fingers before their mouths !

Decidedly, all these ceremonies, probably destined to impress people with awe and expectation, were lost on me. I considered them rather boring and disrespectfully thought of a circus.

Someone passed carrying an Occidental easy-chair. They seemed to arrange the audience-room specially for me.

A few minutes later—it was perhaps twenty minutes past three—one of the secretaries solemnly announced in whispers, "Will you please come into the presence of the Ruler?"

I left the ante-room, which was full of costly vases and expensive carpets, and entered a somewhat smaller room where the Exalted Jewel or Prince of Light was seated in a corner.

He rose when I entered, met me about half-way, and gave me his left hand with great cordiality. "The left one is nearer to the heart," he said smilingly, in excellent English. The Prince of Light, as Narbu told me afterwards, speaks and writes six languages perfectly, viz. Tibetan, English, French, Chinese, Hindustani, and Sanscrit.

I sat down in the Western easy-chair that had been specially brought in for the audience and made myself just as comfortable as if I had been in the parlour of a man of small means who would casually invite me to visit his house.

"You are a man of great capacity," said the Prince, "and you will have to fulfil a great mission in this incarnation. The next few days will be of vital importance to you. The experience and portent of a whole series of lives will be crowded for you into the space of hours. You are called upon to take perhaps the greatest decision you have ever been called upon to make, not only in this life but also in hundreds of previous existences. No one can force your hands. You yourself must make your decision in perfect freedom."

He talked like a king or emperor. Every word seemed to have its portent, and he seemed to be fully conscious of the formidable power he wielded. If Narbu was right, I was in the presence of one of the greatest Powers on earth.

His voice was refined, strong, and beautiful, but had a slightly metallic sound. It was very deep too.

He was very tall and had a long white beard. He looked like a mixture of Pythagoras with a slightly Jewish touch and a refined modern Tibetan belonging to the aristocracy of the country.

When our eyes met I had the strange feeling as of something in me fleeing away from him with great eagerness, but it was only an inexplicable reflex, and since I had had so many conflicting and contradictory spiritual experiences ever since I had come to the Holy City, I paid no further attention to it.

We talked about our respective spheres of activity, my expeditions and my plays.

"You have an iron *will*," he observed, "but this is not enough. You sometimes accomplish things because of your boundless energy. That is not enough. You must acquire the power to make your environment *obey* you." He mentioned two Sanscrit words to illustrate the difference between wanting a thing and *commanding* a thing to come your way.

He seemed to prompt me to try to put myself on a

level with the Creator! I, on the other hand, knew that my greatest asset in life had been a capacity to live fully, to be a creature—a powerful creature in my own way—but yet a child of the Creator, and I had never tried to be like the Maker by "*commanding things to come my way*".

We then talked about spiritual mistakes. He said that "they did not matter". If a man stumbles and falls, he seemed to imply, he would rise again.

It occurred to me that there was at least *one* dreadful mistake in the spiritual realm. If man throws his soul away he cannot make amends for it. He cannot take it back afterwards. There are mistakes which are fatal for all eternity!

If a man jumps from a skyscraper he may undo in a few seconds all he has built up in a lifetime, I thought.

I rather disliked his saying that "a mistake never mattered, for one can make amends for it". I knew that there *are* mistakes for which making amends is impossible. I felt as if this had been said to rush my decision, and immediately the "lion temperament" in me began to assert itself.

From spiritual mistakes the conversation drifted to the question of "power".

"You could become all-powerful," he observed meaningly.

"At what price?" I asked.

"That you must discover for yourself," he answered.

We talked about his Brotherhood. He illustrated how impersonal he was. The individual often disappeared before his eyes. He then only saw principles at work. And great principles they were. Guests did not always realize this.

"Sometimes guests come here who have sacrificed everything for doing so and who go hungry for weeks to be able to come here. Let them be hungry. It is good for them to be hungry," he said with cold emphasis.

I looked at him as he sat there in his costly robes. He seemed to sense what was going on within me.

"I hope you do not misunderstand me," he added, and changed the topic. Our conversation gradually touched deeper problems, such as the contrast between East and West, bloody wars and catastrophes of Nature, and how all these things had deeper causes. He even touched on the problem of politics, dictatorships,* and mass rule, and seemed to be *against* sport !

As I never touch in my books and lectures on any problem which is directly or indirectly connected with politics, I shall withhold the details.

I thought I had already overstepped the time allowed for the audience, and meant to close it by making a few polite remarks about my refusal to put on the ceremonial robe made of black silk.

Then he smiled for the first time.

"You are the first person who has ever entered this part of the palace in clothes like this. I hope you will now realize how little value we really attach to matters of pomp and circumstance."

---

* I mentioned *Coriolanus*, by Shakespeare, and found that he knew it very thoroughly, since he expressed his opinion in a very circumstantial way and also gave a considerable number of details showing that he must have read the play several times.

I sincerely wished I could believe him, but I couldn't.

Suddenly I *felt* that many people were waiting outside as the time allotted to them had arrived. I positively *knew* they were waiting. As explained before, the atmosphere of the City developed these faculties in a strange manner.

I rose and wished to withdraw, but he requested me to stay, saying that he greatly appreciated our conversation. I thanked him and sat down again.

I casually mentioned my future plans and was anxious to find out what he would do under such and such circumstances.

"I never give advice to anybody," he said.

I then broached the subject of religious ceremonies, and after having talked for a while about these matters I asked his permission to attend divine service in the temple on the condition that I should be present as a visitor and on the understanding that my attending it should not imply any obligation to the Occult Brotherhood.

He granted permission, adding that for the first time in the history of the temple I would be allowed to attend a service without putting on a black silk robe.* Furthermore, as a special favour I was also authorized to visit the library-room in the residential-buildings where guests who have not yet become members of the Brotherhood are practically never admitted.

I thanked him and withdrew, respectfully greeted

---

* A "major" black silk robe is worn at special festivals, and at the audiences of the Prince. A "minor" black silk robe is worn at ordinary divine services. Only the Ruler can grant exceptions.

by all the Court officials and Masters of Ceremony when I passed outside the many persons whose receptions I had delayed by the excessively long audience.

I left the palace and walked back to the guest-house. I sent a servant to Narbu, informing him that I had had a long and interesting audience with the Ruler, that I should not come to dinner but would attend divine service the same evening, since I had obtained permission to do so from the Exalted Jewel.

When the servant came to announce that dinner was ready I let him repeat his mechanical formula several times, then I bolted the door and prepared my own meal. After dinner I slept for several hours, and about ten minutes before eleven o'clock in the evening joined Narbu. We both walked over to the temple-building to attend the daily service in the temple.

I briefly told him about the audience, but he seemed to have been informed of it already.

"I hope you are convinced by now that the Exalted Jewel is a powerful spiritual leader," he observed.

"Yes," I replied, holding back the opinion that I still had to find out about him the most important fact, viz. whether he served the cause of Light or the cause of Shadow.

The whole evening I had been in the grip of grave doubts as to the real nature of the whole Brotherhood of Light.

It was dark night when we passed the circular wall surrounding the shaft in the centre of the Holy City.

"This shaft must be very deep," I observed.

"How do you know it is a shaft?" asked Narbu.

"I have explored it a little," I answered.

He seemed greatly surprised.

"It is immeasurably deep," he observed, "but no one except the Prince of Light and a few of the highest Initiates who are called Lords of Compassion know where it leads to. Anyone who would find out where it leads to and what it is used for would have to die. . . . There are such secrets."

"Who would kill him?"

"No one. He would die automatically the following night."

We arrived at the temple building and descended the staircase. The small hall in front of the golden double door leading to the temple was dimly lit by torches held by servants, none of whom was allowed to enter the holy *Lha-Kang*.*

There were several servants helping the members to take off their shoes. They knelt down before them and washed their feet. Services had to be attended bare-footed. Other servants sprayed the naked feet of the hierophants with an abundant supply of perfume. I could not help smiling.

A Master of Ceremonies dressed in black silk distributed the ceremonial robes to the templegoers. They were somewhat simpler than the ones I had seen in the palace, but somewhat smaller and embroidered with silver. When I looked at these people going in such robes to the service I thought of a requiem said in a Catholic church.

Court officials had informed the Master of

---
* House of God.

Ceremonies that I was allowed to enter without putting on a black silk robe and without taking off my shoes.

It was quite an exceptional thing that such a permit had been granted by the Ruler. Later, during the service, I must have looked like a bright spot in the darkness. Everybody else was dressed in black silk. I was the only person present who wore a *chu-pa** of the cheapest kind which was made of cotton and remarkably light in colour.

After having been thoroughly fumigated by a servant armed with a perfume-sprayer, I passed the outer door of the temple. It was a few minutes to eleven.

Another Master of Ceremonies, armed with a substantial-looking stick inlaid with gold and precious stones and having a human skull at the top, approached and informed me in whispers that it was strictly forbidden to talk or even to whisper inside the temple, and that it was considered a serious offence even to look at the other participants in the service. He hoped I would comply with these rules. The alternative—he added this with the greatest politeness—was a respectful and humble request to leave the temple immediately. He bowed almost obsequiously, and I passed the inner door of the temple.

I should like to mention in this connection that bows in the Holy City are quite different from the usual Tibetan greetings. People in the City practically never raise their folded hands to their foreheads, mouths, and hearts, which is frequently seen else-

---

* Gown.

where; and also the Tibetan prostration commonly called *kyagtshagg* is only used during divine service in the Holy City.

The "House of God" measured about twenty-five yards by forty. There were nine large doors in the three walls opposite and right and left from the entrance. They stood wide open, and one could see that they gave access to nine underground tunnels at least several hundred yards long and running out slightly downhill into the bowels of the earth as far as the eye could see.

A kind of altar with a perpetual light burning on it stood in the centre of the temple, and four long tables ran out from this centre forming a large cross. The hierophants sat at these tables. I wanted to sit near Narbu, but the places were assigned by Masters of Ceremony and no participant in the service had the right to choose his place himself. About two hundred members were present already when I took the seat assigned to me.

The walls of the temple were adorned with inscriptions in Tibetan, and I spent quite a few minutes in reading them. I understood some of them, but failed to understand others.

One of them read, "Give your soul to the Master and He will show you the light." I thought of a man buying a cat in a bag.

Another one read, "Distrust your brain. Deep understanding is beyond intelligence."

This only increased my desire to trust my brain.

Another inscription ran, "Blessed be you who suffer. Come to me and I will give you relief."

And another, "Everything is unreal, only my

own words are real." This inscription, I thought irreverently, was none too modest.

The service began by the ringing of bells. The effect of this peal of bells rung far away in the underground tunnels was prodigious. Then a very high Initiate wearing a costly white silk robe solemnly walked up from the northern wall of the temple towards the central altar. His train was held by several minor Initiates. He performed queer rites and movements, his assistants touching the ground behind him with their heads most of the time. The audience alternately rose to their feet like a well-trained body of soldiers, then sat down again or touched the ground with their heads. These three poses alternated in fairly rapid succession.

Bells were rung from time to time, and incense was burned repeatedly. On one occasion the priest walked round the altar seven times, swinging the incense-burner all the time. Towards the end of the service, small pills made of rice were consecrated by the priest and the members of the Brotherhood, one by one, walked up to the altar and each took a consecrated pill from a golden plate and swallowed it with great devotion, walking back to his seat immediately afterwards.

Towards the end of the service an Initiate who carried a silver receptacle came out from one of the tunnels and handed it to the priest, who put it on the altar, consecrated it with great profusion of *sung-pos*,* and then poured out its contents into several hundred small vases, apparently made of

---

* Magical signs.

pure gold, and held up to him on trays by the assistants.

I strained my eyes a little to find out something about the nature of the liquid while it was being poured out. It was blood red! Narbu told me afterwards that it actually was blood! When I asked him *what* kind of blood, he said he was not allowed to answer.

Then the procession started again, the hierophants one by one going up to the altar and emptying the contents of one vase each with great devotion.

This closed the service. There was a mighty peal of underground bells, and the priest and his assistants who bore his train withdrew in a cere-monious fashion and entered the central tunnel in the northern wall of the temple, after having sprinkled the audience with an abundant supply of holy water.

The Brothers walked out in solemn procession, none of them daring to look at anyone else. When going out I noticed that the lower part of all the walls of the temple was an uninterrupted succession of silver-edged glass cases entirely filled with human bones. A rapid calculation showed that the temple contained so-and-so many truckloads of human bones.

Needless to say, I had not gone up to the altar, and had merely stood up and sat down from time to time out of politeness.

After a short talk with Narbu I went to bed. It was about midnight.

I slept deeply, and about ten o'clock in the morning I set out for a long walk in the neighbour-hood. I took along some food, intending to return in the afternoon ; I felt quite fit and by noon I was at a distance of at least seven and a half miles from the City when I heard the rumble of thunder in the distance.

I had left my tent in the Holy City, and for the first time during my travels in Tibet I had nothing to protect myself from a Tibetan thunderstorm, which usually is very violent.

When I had walked back a few miles towards the City I was overtaken by the thunderstorm. There was absolutely nothing that could have been used to afford shelter, so all I could do was to lie down flat on the ground and wait for the storm to pass.

The thunderstorm was unusually violent. Flashes of lightning followed one another in rapid succession and after about five minutes I was literally drenched to the skin. As I dislike walking about in drenched clothes I stripped them off, made a bundle of everything I had on me, and greatly enjoyed this unexpected showerbath. Fortunately there was no hail, and after about half an hour the thunderstorm had passed and the sun came out. I wrung out my clothes and spread them out. It was about 1 p.m. The temperature in the sun was something like fifty degrees Centigrade, and in the intense heat the clothes dried with remarkable rapidity. By about three they were fairly dry. I put them on and, after a meal of *tsamba** soaked in water, walked back to the City.

Those of my readers who are versed in occultism may know that there is no better "occult disinfectant" than water, and especially water coming

---

* Barley meal.

down from the sky. It washes away all magnetic currents sent into one's body and into one's clothes by outward agents. Water absorbs magnetic currents with great eagerness.* It is an occult purifier *par excellence.*†

The thunderstorm must have "demagnetized" me, if I may use that word, and washed away most of the magical currents which had no doubt been brought to bear on me during the last few days.

When I had returned to the City it seemed to me as if my capacity to view things in an absolutely matter-of-fact way had considerably increased.

I went to the residential-building of the members of the Brotherhood where guests were not allowed to enter. When I arrived, I found that the Superintendent had already been informed that the Prince of Light had granted permission for me to visit the library where usually only members of the Fraternity are admitted. Organization in the City seemed to be faultless. Nothing was ever overlooked. Everything seemed to be planned and organized and

---

* It is a well-known fact that various dogmatic religions, such as the Catholic Church and Lamaistic Buddhism, discouraged the practice of bathing for many centuries. In the Middle Ages the Catholic Church took up a vigorous stand against the "immoral" practice of bathing, and the lamas up to this day greatly encourage the fear of water entertained by the Tibetan multitude when the use of water is recommended for cleansing the body. One may wonder whether these organized religions took or take such an attitude because they realize that human bodies are "demagnetized" and cleaned of certain occult currents by the practice of bathing, thus making it more difficult for them to maintain their spiritual control of the multitude. As far as the Catholic Church is concerned, they are a much too practical body to maintain an attitude which would seem too incongruous with the period in which we live. That is why the Catholic Church now no longer takes a stand against bathing, but the lamas still do so.

† That is why it is used for making Holy Water in temples and churches.

recorded.   Things in an ant-hill could not work more smoothly, I thought.

Narbu happened to be in the library, and rose to greet me.

The walk, the neutral atmosphere outside the City, and the good "wash-up" seemed to have increased my capacity to examine things objectively.

Narbu's eyes seemed to have become a little more lifeless.   It was as if an occult magneto had drawn out of him all that was best in him ; his soul, his freedom, his personality.   I listened to his voice. It sounded metallic and more soulless than it had sounded in his *dsong*.

I told him that I had been out for a walk.

While I talked to him I began to listen to the sound of my own voice.   It had a metallic and "coated" touch too.   It was not hoarseness—oh no, it was a much more dreadful thing.

I left Narbu, who was studying a manuscript written in Sanscrit, and went over to a mirror. When I saw myself I stepped back aghast.   Never before had I seen my eyes, the "windows of the soul", gazing so lifelessly.   Where was I ?   There was something strange about my features too. There was something of the grin of a demon in them.   What did all that mean ?

I walked round the circular library building, brilliantly lit by the daylight flooding in through the ceiling.   I examined the pictures on the walls. There were reproductions of various "Soul Saviours" and "Redeemers" of past ages ; there were pictures which seemed to be enlarged reproductions of the "Supreme Jewel" and his foremost lieutenants.

I looked into their eyes. They were beautiful but gloomy. All was there, intelligence, power, but no—soul! Everything in me cried out in one wild agony. I sat down and put my hands before my face. I had recognized the nature of all these saviours of souls. They were—fallen angels!

They were angels who had lost their glory because they had wanted to be like God. And when they had thus precipitated themselves into the bottomless abyss from which there is no return, just like a mountain-climber who makes a dash to soar to the sun but falls down into the abyss, the fallen angels *turned against the Creator* and now live for the purpose of making others share their dreadful fate by dragging them down with them into the abyss.

The Prince of Light was really the Prince of Darkness in disguise!

The few minutes following this realization were the most dreadful of my life. My whole being cried out in spiritual agony. Outwardly I was quiet and composed, but inwardly I was in the grip of a spiritual storm shaking the very foundations of my being. So intense was my agony that it is beyond the power of words to convey a description of it. Only people who have had a glimpse of the spiritual can realize what the term "soul agony of the greatest intensity" really means.

It was as if the experience of hundreds of incarnations, the suffering of whole existences, was concentrated into the space of a few minutes of spiritual anguish.   So intense was my agony that it must have disturbed the whole psychical atmosphere of the City of the Initiates.   I now positively felt powerful magnetic currents rushing on me from all sides to extinguish this newly acquired spiritual realization.

A door opened and the Prince entered the library attended by only two secretaries.   Everybody rose to his feet.*   He came up to me.

"Have you taken your decision?" he asked in a beautiful but dreadfully hollow and metallic voice.

"Yes," I answered firmly.

He blew one mighty breath right into my face.

"Confounded sorcerer," I thought, "now you reveal your real nature!"†

"Step back—in the name of the Creator!" I almost shouted in a mighty voice.   I think never before had I heard my own voice so full of vigour and soul-power.   My whole being *fused into one indissoluble unit*, and my whole self lay in that voice.

The Ruler recoiled.   He then briskly turned and left the library.

I suddenly realized that the penalty for recognizing the real nature of such a being must be death.

---

* I have explained before that the palace was connected with the other buildings by subterranean passages.   The Prince could thus reach any other part of the Underground City in a few minutes.

† Blowing into another man's face is a certain characteristic of demons or their servants or disciples incarnated in the flesh.   By these means they try to get hold of their man and obtain a good basis for subsequent magical operations destined to deprive him of his free will.   The best *spiritual* armour against this dreadful practice is an iron will, intense I- and Soul-Consciousness, and the mental attitude of "may the Creator punish you for that" without hatred!   The best *physical* remedy against blows by demons is the eating of beans, bread prepared with much yeast, and similar kinds of food which produce abundant gases inside the body.

Having failed to snatch my soul while I was alive and had the protective shield of my intelligence, he would no doubt try to murder me by occult practices as it might be easier for him to snatch my soul "on the other side".

I had always possessed courage. Once a gun had gone off a few inches from my face, the bullet passing my nose, but friends had assured me that I had hardly moved my eyelashes. I have been to the most deserted parts of the world alone, carrying my own food to last fifteen days when I knew that a sprained ankle or some other minor accident would mean certain death. I have been face to face with death many times without showing the slightest emotion.

But now it was a different matter. I was not fighting for life, but for my soul !

It was as if a bottomless abyss had opened before my feet and a cold hand tried to tear open my heart and to draw me away from the Creator for ever.

For the first time in my life I fled in terror. When running out to reach my room to fetch my belongings and leave the City, never to return, I made the mistake of running towards the sanitation-building instead of the guest-house. (As said before, all the "buildings" in the city were alike from outside.) I ran downstairs, passing with lightning rapidity through the two corridors corresponding to the ones I used to take when going to my room in the guest-house.

I had not realized that I was in the wrong building, and when two servants got up to stop me I simply pushed them aside with as little violence as was absolutely necessary* and opened a door.

I was in the "kitchen" of the City, to which no one except the kitchen staff and the highest Initiates had access.

A human corpse lay in the centre of the kitchen. Lifeless and automatonlike "cooks" cut off small pieces of flesh. Ten or fifteen large pans made of massive silver were suspended over so many fires apparently fed with alcohol, and the pieces of human flesh were passed on to boards where they were carefully cut up into small pieces.

It was not quite certain, of course, that the contents of the silver pans were destined for the members and guests of the Holy City, but the very possibility of my having partaken of such food was dreadful. If human flesh was actually mixed into our food it was small wonder that it had disagreed with me.

The cooks gave a mighty stare at the intruder, but two or three seconds were enough to have a look at the whole kitchen, and I immediately rushed back to the guest-house.

Narbu had followed me from the library. He had lost sight of me and now anxiously looked round in all directions while he stood before the guest-house.

"Wait here, please," I cried, and a minute later I was back with my belongings, including the urine-bottle, which I did not want to leave behind as I realized that it would provide an excellent basis for magical operations directed against me.

---

* I always avoid unnecessary harshness.

Narbu accompanied me out of the City to the slabs displaying the inscription, "Border". After all, it was he who had invited me, and it was up to him to see me safely to the precincts of the City.

"So you are going," said Narbu sadly.

The poor, kind-hearted man! He thought he was in the city of a Great Light Power, and the thought that I did not want "salvation" made him sad.

For a moment I contemplated whether I should tell him bluntly that he really was in the city of the Evil One, but strange to say I felt that I could not.

For spiritual realizations entail enormous spiritual responsibilities.

Even the Powers of Evil have their spiritual mission. They snatch souls if men themselves give them up. By his *spiritual* sins* man himself weakens the ties which link him to his soul, and the more he sins spiritually the more he strikes himself with blindness until he can no longer see the difference between "God" and the Creator, no matter how high are his occult accomplishments. The devil tempts, but he can only seize souls that voluntarily yield to his temptation.

That is a law of the universe. I felt I could save no one from the Evil One. By telling Narbu that the Exalted Jewel was identical with the Prince of Darkness I should have influenced his spiritual attitude and interfered with his spiritual destiny, which lay in his own hands. I felt I had no right to do that, for the supreme spiritual law is absolutely

---

* Using the impersonal for personal uses (selfish prayers) and wanting to be like God are the two most frequent spiritual sins.

free choice by every individual.   Man himself can choose resplendent light, but he himself can also throw himself down into the bottomless abyss from whence there is no return.

Oh, the dreadful tragedies of spiritual life !

There stood Narbu, kind-hearted and only afflicted with a slight dose of spiritual arrogance, but otherwise good at the core.   He wanted to save me, although it was he himself who needed salvation, and I could not save him.   I had to leave him to his fate.   I felt the dreadful tragedy of the moment when I greeted him and went on my way.

Just as the tiniest creature has its mission in the universe, every spiritual force, be it one belonging to the upward trend of life or to the downward, has its mission too.   It is bound by spiritual laws which are inherent to its very nature.   No special oath is required to keep it within these bounds.   No spiritual creature can act in a way contrary to its spiritual nature.

God and devil both go their own way.   And the creature can seize at will the upward or downward trend of life.   The more he sins against his soul the more he will strike himself with blindness. But once he goes to his doom no one can save him.

I had been for three days in the City of the Initiates, but the experience of whole decades seemed to have been crowded into these three momentous days.*

---

* Kind-hearted Narbu died suddenly some time after I had left the Holy City.   It was not necessary for me, therefore, to hold back certain secrets out of consideration for him.

CHAPTER V

THE FLIGHT

I TURNED towards the region where my Tibetan hermit friend lived whose brother had procured me Tibetan clothes south of the Gobi Desert. I felt that the Ruler of the Holy City would not feel safe while I lived, and as it was quite impossible for him to have me murdered openly—be it only out of consideration for Narbu, whose eyes might have been opened by such an occurrence—he would no doubt try to kill me by powerful magical operations.

Even attacks of this kind become more difficult when the distance separating the magician from his enemy increases, and as I had no desire to fight these currents more than was absolutely necessary, I intended to set out at the rate of about thirty miles a day and take a rest upon my arrival in the abode of the wise hermit.

It was late in the evening, and as soon as night had fallen I put up my tent at a place about eight miles distant from the Underground City. I naturally chose a place where I was hidden by small ridges.

I knew that the magical attacks I had to expect would in all probability be brought to bear during the night, about twelve to one being the worst hours, and that so long as I remained awake and fully conscious of my physical surroundings their effect would be automatically minimized.

I had been exposed to such magical influences on former occasions, but I realized that those had been merely child's play compared with what I had to expect from expert magicians welded into one powerful secret brotherhood headed by the Prince of Darkness in person.

I kept awake all night and only felt some strange pangs in the left side of my chest just above the heart. The reader may imagine that I had ample food for thought throughout that night.

There was adventure crowded into the space of a little over two weeks which could have amply filled several lives. I really was glad to have these quiet hours to digest so many spiritual experiences.

Then I thought of beautiful Dolma and the dreadful tragedy of my being unable to save her or anyone else from the clutches of the soul-snatching Prince.

In the small hours I felt very sleepy and for the fraction of a second I lost full consciousness. In that short moment of half-consciousness I heard the noise of a wooden lid being closed just above me. I started and regained full consciousness. I felt that the magicians were at work. They were "burying" me in the City. As I had left nothing behind, they had possibly got hold of the piece of paper on which I had written those few words in Tibetan letters on my arrival in the guest-house. So they had at least one thing, one "basis", for their magical operations. They were possibly "burying" the slip in my place, at the same time focusing on me their whole attention,* and performing a regular funeral with elaborate rites.

Soon before sunrise I folded my tent, but when I was just about to start and had come on top of the small elevation behind the place where I had spent the night I saw that a procession of people was moving in my direction. I instantly stooped and made for the deepest hollow that was to be found within a radius of a hundred yards. There I quickly dug myself into the sand.

A quarter of an hour later the procession was quite near. What on earth were these people doing here at half past five in the morning? The procession had moved in the direction of the Underground City, and to my great astonishment a few people came in the opposite direction from the City of the Initiates.

The procession arrived at the nearest hollow about eighty yards from the place where I had dug myself in and waited for the people coming from the City. I looked at their clothes, which seemed to be familiar. They were servants from the City carrying bodies lying on a kind of stretcher. A few of them walked behind dressed as Tibetan *lag-pas*†.

So some of the Prince's lieutenants were corpse-cutters! Was it possible that they took the corpses

---

* I may say that this "magic" must really have had some effect. For when I arrived amongst the hermits about ten days later they said there was a strong cadaveric smell about me. I had smelt it myself, but as I am always inclined to attribute "marvels" to the subjective element, I had thought this was due to auto-suggestion. My wise friends then gave me much garlic to eat (garlic is very rare and expensive, but forms part of the pharmacy of the wise men of Tibet).

† "Hands" or corpse-cutters.

from families living in the district, and instead of cutting them up they had devised some trick to steal the dead bodies and smuggle them into the City under the cover of night ?

The people coming *from* the City had arrived. I recognized them by their resplendent black robes. They were Masters in the Occult Brotherhood. They knelt down near the lifeless bodies and then magical operations were started to "resuscitate" them. I am sorry I must withhold a few details relative to these practices, for some of the operations were so disgusting that I must abstain from giving a description, be it even in Latin.

After strenuous "work" greatly varying in duration, three of the lifeless bodies had begun to move and walked on towards the City mechanically, like so many robots, led on by one of the Masters. Were the lifeless bodies really dead before the resuscitation practices were started ? If so, it was dreadful to imagine what kind of servants had cleaned my room and prepared the food in the Holy City !

Five other lifeless bodies where the resuscitation practices had failed to take effect were carried on towards the Holy City. Being of a practical disposition, the Exalted Jewel possibly did not wish to lose a single lifeless body he had obtained by trickery or by bribery. Those which were past hope may have been sent to the kitchen and their bones to the temple. Dreadful !

As soon as the procession, preceded by the walking robots led by the Masters, had disappeared from sight, I approached to ascertain whether the stretchers and numerous footsteps had left some traces on the ground. The experience had been so unusual that I wished to check up whether I could believe the evidence of my senses. After inspecting the footprints very thoroughly, I marched on.

Why on earth did these people perform those dreadful ceremonies in broad daylight? They had a whole Underground City where they could do all they liked, surrounded as they were by walking automatons who could never betray them. And even if such ceremonies could not be performed underground for some reason or other, why did they perform them in broad daylight? True, the chances of meeting someone in that forlorn part were exceedingly small, but, small as they were, why did they run that risk at all?

Thinking further along these lines while I walked on, I came to the conclusion that if such clever rogues took any chances at all they must have had an imperative reason for doing so.

The "waking-up" ceremonies were performed in the light of the sun that had just risen. This seemed to indicate that the cosmical currents they needed for their dreadful purpose reached their greatest intensity soon after sunrise. Sunrise and noon are the hours of God, sunset and midnight the hours of darkness. The devils stole cosmic forces from the Creator, then, to accomplish their own horrible work.

As usual, the Evil One is strongest when he snatches away the forces of the Creator and uses divine forces to his own end.

Of course, all these speculations were based on

the assumption that the *lag-pas** had really escorted dead bodies.

I walked on at top speed, and once more reviewed the happenings of the last three days.

Why had I been saved?

I had come to the City on the invitation and recommendation of Narbu, who was himself misled and failed to realize the real nature of the Brotherhood. I had entered the City in a disinterested spirit *to help and not in order to get something*. My lion temperament had revolted when they proposed to hang round me the black ceremonial robes which were in all probability magnetized too. All their subtle magic, mesmerized food and maybe even other tricks I knew nothing about, had failed to produce the occult results they desired, because throughout my stay in the City I had never sinned, be it even in thought. The Evil One can only take those who give themselves voluntarily up to him, and where he oversteps that limit there are angels of the Creator who protect the innocent.

They had tried to snatch my soul away! I love my soul, through which the Creator speaks to me through my heart. The harder they worked to snatch it away the more desperately I clung to it.

Great fires, like other turmoils in life, may destroy the weak, but they purify the strong and make him still stronger. More and more I began to be aware of the fact that life, including life on spiritual planes, was not an affair of peaceful contemplation and quiet worship, but a dreadful turmoil, a grim fight, and a bitter struggle.

---

* Corpse-cutters.

Had I met this procession three days earlier carrying lifeless bodies on stretchers it might have opened my eyes at once. I might have immediately realized the real nature of the Brotherhood and thus missed the greatest experience of my life.

The following two days were marked by all sorts of minor and greater troubles. I was attacked by whole swarms of gnats, and during the night, while I lay on the ground wide awake—I have stated earlier why I had to sacrifice sleep—I heard a succession of queer noises in the darkness. There was a scamper and a continual coming and going resembling the sounds you hear in a warehouse infested by thousands of large rats. In the morning I found that practically all my food had been eaten during the night and even my equipment damaged by bites such as could only be attributed to rats of unusual size.

The subsequent night I had the dreadful experience with murderous parasites which I have described in my earlier book. I might have bled to death had I not noticed the creatures in time. This was the third night since I had left the City, and for the first time since leaving it I had a little sleep, but every time I passed from a state of full consciousness into the state of half-consciousness which usually precedes sleep, I felt as if I lay in a coffin. So I made an effort again and again to return to full consciousness and to keep wide awake until daybreak.

Once more I had plenty of time to think over the dreadful practices and strange resuscitation rites of the soul-snatchers in the City of the Initiates.

What was the fundamental difference between the members of the Brotherhood who had given, or were on the way to give, their souls to the Evil One on the one hand, and those lifeless servants on the other ?

If man really was complex, what did he consist of ?

I, of course, realized the danger of contemplations of that sort. Consciousness, which should be totalitarian in man, then, has a tendency to split up, which is a very real danger. By indulging too much in speculations of this sort, man provides a *point d'appui* for the great spiritual forces forming part of the downward current of life which serve the purpose of *disintegration.**

The physical nature of man is fivefold, I thought. There are five organic systems in our bodies to which all organic functions of the body can be related ; man has five senses ; he has five fingers on each hand and five toes on each foot—five seems to be the number of the creature and of man in particular. But even if we look beyond the physical aspect of man, his nature seems to be fivefold. Man is a unit composed of purely physical characteristics, sensation, feeling, intelligence, and will. So why should he not be composed of five different vehicles welded into one unit which man does very well not to try to dissociate under any circumstances ? (I thought of the dreadful crime against himself and his soul committed by the *sungmi* in the Tibetan monastery—see Chapter II of this book—and of Tibetan séances

---

* The Shiwa principle of the Hindus. By the way, "*Achi*" means "to die" in Tibetan, and "*shi*" means "dead".

when people voluntarily relinquish control over all the vehicles that rightfully belong to them, thus throwing themselves open to all sorts of disembodied entities, just like a man who might throw open his doors and windows during the night in a house built in the jungle !)

The difference between the members of the Brotherhood and the lifeless servants resuscitated by magical practices was the following, I thought :

The Brothers had given their souls to the Evil One. They were men composed of a body, sensation, feeling, and intelligence. Only their will was no longer their own. They had given up their most divine attribute, their free will, to the Evil One.

The servants, on the other hand, I thought, were mere robots. When "they" had died, their subtler vehicles had left their corpses immediately after death and only their dense body remained, their vitalizing principle which is the seat of sensation floating about near the corpse. Then the body was stolen, and the vitalizing principle made to re-enter it. The servants, then, were mere, agglomerates of a body plus a vehicle of sensation, that is to say mere robots possessing a body and sensation, but devoid of feeling, intelligence, and will.*

Dreadful as this body-snatching practice was, it seemed to be infinitely less tragic than the soul-snatching business going on in the Holy City, for the souls of the men who had inhabited the

---

* My whole experience in the City confirmed this opinion. The servants had no intelligence at all. They mechanically repeated certain formulae. They were absolutely devoid of the capacity to think independently and to have emotions. They were body plus sensation and nothing else. In a sense they were ideal servants !

bodies of the servants were not affected by the fact that their dead bodies had been stolen by the lieutenants of the Prince.

Daybreak had come and I rose to march on.

I had another strenuous and unpleasant day.

By "coincidence" I lost my whole water-supply early in the morning. There was no thunderstorm all day. The afternoon was hotter than usual and I suffered greatly from thirst. With parched lips I lay down in the afternoon and fell asleep. It was nearly nightfall when I awoke. I felt marvellously refreshed. I felt glad, since I had a better chance to keep awake during the time when those confounded magical practices started soon after midnight.

The following day I visited one of the monasteries I have mentioned in my earlier book, and again, by "coincidence", I had one of my worst experiences. I was nearly found out by the lamas and had to face the ordeal of sitting about motionless for many hours until I could make my escape.

Another monastery was visited two days later.

As is customary in Tibetan monasteries, I was offered holy water to drink. It was impossible to refuse, as all the other pilgrims seemed to be very keen on drinking the holy water, which was offered by a kind of verger.* Had I refused, I might have attracted much unwelcome attention. An hour later the holy water produced a very unwelcome reaction† as far as my physical well-

---

* These vergers, by the way, get the lion's share of the coins "collected" from pious pilgrims in Tibetan monasteries.

† I know that the *utpa-lam-dag* (castor oil plant) is known at least in southern Tibet, but I do not suspect the vergers to be so ingenious as to add castor oil to the holy water in order to make some money afterwards by providing certain facilities.

being was concerned, and since the sanitary arrangements in the monastery did not provide the necessary degree of privacy which a Westerner expects as his natural right on certain occasions, an unusual amount of skill and dexterity and all my resourcefulness were required to wriggle out of the difficulty, since I was in the disguise of a Tibetan and had dyed my face and hands only, since my supply of colour was exceedingly limited.

I then spent a few hours quietly walking about in the monastery. As I was "deaf and dumb", in order to hide my foreign accent, I also enjoyed the priceless advantage of not being pestered by the many guides who prey on pilgrims in the Tibetan monasteries, no matter how poor they may be, as they seem to know by experience that the religious poor are always only too glad to let go of their last farthing for religious purposes. I thought how wise Western tourists would be if they adopted the clever practice of posing as "deaf and dumb" persons when visiting certain guide-infested tourist centres.

I had a good look at the Tibetan butter idols. There were idols in the monastery entirely composed of butter mixed with coloured earth. They, of course, stood in the shadow, since the afternoons in the summer are dreadfully warm. I had to smile once more when thinking of the fact that idols fight shy of sunshine, since the latter had a tendency to melt them. Was it not symbolical, I thought, that idols could only exert their influence in the shadow and not in bright sunshine!

Elaborate ceremonies were performed by the

lamas. An abundant supply of human bones had been used for making censers and other objects used for divine service.

I thought of the Holy City. The same spirit seemed to reign in the monastery, although in a greatly diluted manner.

The lamas distributed pills made of rice to the pilgrims after having consecrated them by elaborate rites. I thought of the temple in the City.

The lamas *also* spoke of the necessity to *believe blindly* in the contents of their 333 holy books.* Just like the members of the Brotherhood in the City, I thought. There, too, the most sublime gift of man—his intelligence—had to be discarded and transcended.

They continually spoke, too, of "salvation", of "saving" one's soul by giving it up to the Divine. Many, perhaps most, of the conversations at which I had been present in the City—in the dining-building and elsewhere—had a distinct parallel in the sermons of the lamas. The Prince catered for the elect, the lamas for the multitude, I thought, but I failed to see any *fundamental* difference between the two.

And God's sun shone over the monastery.

I thought of the dreadful tragedy of a world in open revolt against its Creator.

---

* The holy books of dogmatic Buddhism consist of the 108 volumes of the *Kandjur* and the 225 volumes of the *Tandjur*, making a total of 333 volumes. In occult numerology (philosophy of abstract figures) the total of the various figures composing a number plays an important part. If we examine the above three numbers we find that the sum of the figures composing the numbers 108, 225, and 333 is nine in each case. The reader will remember that I mentioned earlier in the book that in the City of the Initiates *nine* was considered an especially auspicious number !

I spent a few hours studying the mechanism of meditation which I have described in an earlier book, and then left the monastery with much sadness in my heart.

Were not nearly all these poor people in the same position as Narbu? They wanted to be "saved" and tried to "save" others. And while they were looking for "salvation" their poor beings disintegrated more and more! Their soul-consciousness decreased. Oh, the dreadful tragedy of being unable to help them!

Trouble followed trouble. It was as if some mysterious hand was putting obstacles in my way. The following morning I met with a gang of brigands. I saw them too late, and when they searched my belongings they confiscated one of the things I needed most: a thin blanket made of fine wool. None of the many brigands I had met earlier had had the heart to take the blanket away from me, who to all appearances was a poor lonely traveller. But these brigands were tougher and much less considerate. I had a faint idea that they were really lamas and carried on the brigand profession as a sideline. On another occasion I had recognized a robber in the robe of a lama when visiting a monastery after having been robbed. The Tibetans hold the lamas in high esteem and do not even dare to look at them, which must greatly facilitate this double profession.

I wonder whether the 108 holy books of the *Kandjur** contain a passage reading "your left hand should ignore what your right hand is doing".

---

* The first part of the Tibetan "bible".

If it does, the lamas may have no difficulty in absolving themselves from the sin of robbery.

I spent one of my worst nights.

I had no blanket and the temperature in the small hours was not much higher than about 18 degrees Fahrenheit. As if by another coincidence the coldest night in many weeks had come on just after my blanket had been confiscated! The cold of such Tibetan nights strikingly contrasts with the generous sunshine and hot weather usually reigning on cloudless summer afternoons. Although I know how to protect myself from cold by keeping my muscles and chest entirely relaxed, there are limits to physical endurance. Lying motionless for hours in an unheated tent at about 18 degrees Fahrenheit when one has no blanket is more than anyone can bear. From time to time I galloped round outside the tent in wide circles, and then lay crumpled up within like a child in the womb of its mother. I had not a wink of sleep all that night.

Then the sun rose, and all was bright again.

Is there anything that symbolizes the Creator better than the sun, which generously gives warmth and life to all those who do not keep out its radiancy by their own free will? The sun is generous and majestic, and yet keeps his distance from those for whom he shines. He who looks full into the sun may be struck with blindness. The same applies to the creature who wants to fathom the Creator. If you wish to be too much like Him, if you wish to reach out into the domain beyond the reach of the creature, you strike yourself with spiritual blindness and mistake the moon for the sun.

I walked on as fast as I could.   I had no blanket, and a few dreadfully cold nights were before me. I was only about 150 miles from the abode of the wise hermit whose brother I had met south of the Gobi Desert.   I had asked the latter whether great spiritual teachers lived on the way so that I might visit them when passing the respective districts.   He had not mentioned the City of which I had learned only through my acquaintance with Dolma and Narbu, but had talked about a great spiritual Teacher to whom I might listen.   He lived on a high mountain which I would pass a few days before reaching the district where several hermits, including his brother, lived.

"Does he serve light or darkness?" I had asked him.

"I cannot tell you that," he had replied.   "You must discover it for yourself."

"Is it not your spiritual duty to warn me of demons who may easily appear in the disguise of angels, as occasionally happens in Western countries?" I had asked further.

"No," he had said.   "Even if I realized their nature myself, it is a man's highest spiritual duty to respect another man's spiritual freedom.   By cataloguing spiritual teachers and telling you who is the evil one and who is not I should influence your spiritual attitude.   You must discover things for yourself.   You are going to Tibet.   *You* have to take the risks, not I."   His answer had been very firm.

I walked all morning, and then slept during many hours in the afternoon.   I awoke feeling a very strange kind of pain in the region of the heart. I examined myself medically in a thorough manner, even devising an emergency stethoscope for the occasion, but found that there was absolutely nothing wrong with me, and I think no specialist, had he been present, could have discovered anything either. Yet the pain was rather violent, as though an invisible hand was directing piercing stabs against my heart. So it was either a case of auto-suggestion (I wished to God it was!) or the work of those confounded sorcerers in the City. I knew that magical processes of this kind lose the largest part of their vigour after five days and eagerly anticipated the time when five clear days would have lapsed since I had left the Holy City.

Evening came, and I greatly regretted the impossibility of walking on in the darkness, since the countryside became more and more mountainous.

After another dreadfully cold night spent in an unheated tent without a blanket at a temperature that was many degrees under freezing-point, I felt so tired that I fell asleep soon after sunrise. Late in the forenoon I again started at top speed and, after having consulted the sketch drawn by the hermit, I knew that only a few miles separated me from the mountain on which the great spiritual Teacher lived.

My hermit friend had told me that he refused to bear any title, that he lived very simply without making any effort at being simple,* that he

---

* Simplicity in itself may be a pose. The author has occasionally found "humble" people to be even more irritating than strutting and blustering folk.

had no special circle of disciples or followers, and that he always stressed the necessity that people should follow the light of their *own* intelligence and not allow themselves to be influenced by anyone else. In short, he seemed to be the very reverse of the Prince in the City and, needless to say, I was rather inclined to consider him as a sincere teacher, although I reserved my opinion until I had actually met him and his followers.

He was known by the name of Gentle Friend, and according to what my hermit friend had told me before I entered Tibet, many Tibetans interested in *Dhul-shugg* principles* were amongst his regular visitors.

About five hundred yards before I reached his abode—the Gentle Friend, as I had been told, never travelled, and was always at home—I met a nice young Tibetan and asked him whether he knew where the *stonpatshempo* (Great Teacher) lived.

"*Lags, lags*,"† he answered, "his *kanpa*‡ is over there. About twenty people live with him here at present, some of them in the *kanpa* and others in *phugs*§ close by. Who has asked you to come here?"

"No one in particular," I answered, "but a friend of mine who lives south of the Gobi Desert mentioned to me his teaching and I am interested in it."

"I at once knew by your accent," he observed, "that you come from very far, and probably from a remote part in the north."

---

* A teaching which recommends the elimination of all passion in life and the cool judging of things in an impersonal way.
† "Yes, yes."   ‡ House.   § A kind of den.

"You are right," I said.

We arrived at the house and I asked to see the Gentle Friend.

I was told that the Teacher had nothing special to say to visitors, but if I was interested in his teaching there was no objection to my listening to a few of his lectures. The Teacher was for everyone and not for private persons. No one stood nearer to the Gentle Friend than anyone in the multitude, and that is why he did not receive visitors. If I wanted to come next morning I should be welcome. I could live in any of the unoccupied dens I liked to choose, and if I had not food and fuel enough I could get some barley-meal and dried yak-dung in the house.

Decidedly, I began to like this place. Everything seemed to be so simple, matter-of-fact, and unobtrusive. It seemed to be the very opposite of that dreadful City.

The following morning I met some of the guests who lived in the other dens. It was a rather motley crowd belonging to various walks of life. There were even a few tradesmen who had come a long way from an important trading centre to stay on the "Mountain of Simplicity". The guests were all deeply interested in religious matters and most of them seemed to be possessed of an unusual amount of intelligence. However, they were not much cleaner than other Tibetans in similar conditions.

"Where is your *kye-sa* ?"* was one of the first questions.

The young man I had met the day before told them

---
* Native place.

all he knew about me. He said that I was a truth-seeker and my attention had been called to the Mountain of Simplicity by a *drog-bzan**, living south of the Gobi Desert. This remark created quite a sensation, since only few people had ever visited the mountain who came from so "enormously distant" a place.

Some people observed that there was a very queer smell about me. I had noticed it myself. It was as if I carried dead mice in my pocket, but I could not help it.

The little crowd was keenly interested in abstract problems. While we were walking up to the *kanpa†* for the lecture they discussed the problems of good and evil, light and shadow, with great animation. For them it seemed good and evil did not exist at all. There was no such thing as "bad", one of them observed, and all the others agreed to it. Everything was a mere reflection of ourselves.

I inwardly disagreed. I thought of the dreadful City I had left a few days before. I knew for a fact that such a thing as evil in itself existed. No amount of philosophy could discuss the devil away and the obvious polarity of nature.

We entered the "House of Simplicity". It was none too clean. We sat down on mattresses. Soon afterwards the room filled up with other people and when about twenty to twenty-five had gathered for the lecture the outer door was closed and bolted and the Gentle Friend,

---

* A good friend.   † House.

whom everyone seemed to regard as a great spiritual teacher, entered.

I compared him with the spiritual head of the City. He seemed to be the very opposite in appearance. Whereas the Prince or Exalted Jewel had been the very picture of majesty, this man seemed to be a picture of humility. He was unostentatiously dressed in a cheap and almost shabby *chupa*. His face was kind and gentle and looked the very embodiment of renouncement, unselfishness, and happiness. He was rather old, and his body perhaps a trifle too stout, his embonpoint in all probability being due to lack of exercise. As I said before, he never travelled.

I had had so many spiritual "surprises" in my life (I had just had the greatest in the City); that I entirely reserved my opinion of him until I had heard him lecture several times, and studied those who listened to him. All this, I imagined, would take several days. As I had a full month left for studying the Tibetan hermits and *respas*,* which was the final stage of my travels in the country, I decided to sacrifice two to three days to find out all about the Gentle Friend, and the Mountain of Simplicity.

The Teacher started his lecture by directing attention to the utter futility of conscious spiritual guidance. Everyone, he said, must be his own spiritual light and his own guide. Spirituality could not be *gton*,† he said, and stressed the

---

* Ascetes who can sit naked and motionless for hours in icily cold weather without freezing to death.

† Given.

word several times. It was always there. Man
had to take it by perfecting himself, and the way
to this perfection was reached by introspection,
that is to say, by understanding oneself and by
discovering the real value of things.

The longer he talked the better I liked him.
There seemed to be so much common sense and
sincerity about this man.

During the lecture enormous rats seemed to
play a kind of football match on the roof of the
house. They greatly disturbed the talk by
doing so, but the Gentle Friend and most of
his listeners loved animals—*all* animals—and did
not allow anyone to fight or chase rats or any
other creature. Non-resistance to everything, as
I learned a little later, was the keynote of their
whole existence, and this non-resistance included
a passive attitude to animals of any kind.

I respectfully disagreed with the Gentle Friend
in this respect. There were obviously two realms
of animals in nature. If I was kind to a horse or a
dog and in exceptional cases even to a bear or a
squirrel, the kindness would be justified. But how
about kindness to parasites, to snakes, to crocodiles
or sharks? The latter animals belonged to a
different branch of life. No amount of love,
kindness, and non-resistance would ever disarm
a shark or a louse, I thought.

Was it not a crime then to eat, because the food
taken by the Gentle Friend and our circle could
have fed many more rats? Surely many of them
were hungry, for rats and other parasitic animals
always multiply a little faster than the food supply

available for them could justify, so that they always need more food.

Life is a struggle. In this struggle, a just and equitable balance can be kept between man and animals of the non-parasitic type, but the animals belonging to the descending branch of life, such as gnats, mosquitoes, rats, mice, flies, etc., must be *fought*.

I wondered whether the Gentle Friend would also object to disinfection during epidemics out of kindness to germs of disease if he happened to come to the West!

However, apart from this disregard for the elementary fact of polarity in life which led to this absurd kindness to rats, I quite agreed with him as to most of what he had said about spiritual matters and the necessity for man to be independent from visible guidance in spiritual matters.

He did not answer any questions after the lecture, but there was considerable discussion amongst the members of the circle after he had left the room.

The Teacher gave a second lecture in the afternoon.

He began by taking a strong stand against asceticism and *bsnen-gnas** to obtain spiritual results, and I again heartily agreed with him. He then took up the subject of magic, and said it was not only a *kun-tag*,† but a veritable crime.

The only way to salvation, he went on, was through the disappearance of *gti-mug*.‡ Man must discard his separate spiritual existence, observed

---

* Fasting.   † Spiritual error.   ‡ Ignorance, stupidity.

the Gentle Friend with great vigour. And this result is reached by introspection, that is to say by giving up what I consider the most Divine thing in man, his *Will* !

The idea struck me that to try to be "like God" by *entirely* destroying one's I-consciousness amounts to committing spiritual suicide. Annihilation could not be the supreme goal of life. Just as in material things as much egotism is justified as is absolutely necessary to maintain our separate existence, it is the duty of the creature to maintain its individuality also in the realm of spirituality, otherwise life would have no meaning.

I profoundly disagreed with the Gentle Friend in this respect, although most of the things he had said in the earlier part of his lecture had been perfectly acceptable.

He then went on discussing (1) I-consciousness, (2) group-consciousness, and (3) Divine consciousness, in which all separate consciousness was absent.

He said that in prehistoric times man was not yet individualized. Man then identified himself with the clan to which he happened to belong. Today man had reached the stage of individual I-consciousness and the next step for him was to go from individual I-consciousness to Divine consciousness.

I again could not help disagreeing.

How could critically minded people swallow such an idea? Prehistoric man was group-conscious. Modern man *is not yet fully I-conscious.* Again and again *he is drawn back into the clan and family spirit*, that is to say, he is *alternately group-*

conscious and I-conscious. So the trend *of evolution in modern man is from group-consciousness towards full I-consciousness.* And now the Gentle Friend proposed that man, whose I-consciousness is just emerging from group-consciousness, should jump back to a state of "total" consciousness which existed *prior* to group-consciousness !

I again thought of the fact that he recommended people to put themselves on a level with the Creator. Once more I realized a short moment of acute spiritual anguish when I realized that this man, too, served the purpose of the fallen angels, and wondered whether he was a mere tool or whether he himself was conscious of his decidedly destructive mission.

How beautiful had been most of these two lectures ! There had been so much truth in them, and yet they were only *nearly* true. The word "almost" in spiritual matters is an ominous one. The Evil One himself is "almost" God, and in this little word "almost" lies all the dreadful difference.

Perhaps the Gentle Friend did not realize himself what he was doing. This prospect was slight, but it existed. There are cases of this kind in spiritual life. It occasionally happens that sincere people are struck with spiritual blindness and serve the cause of darkness while they honestly believe they serve the cause of light.

I returned to my *phug** and sat down to think over the further spiritual lesson I had received, when I had come to realize the real nature of the Gentle Friend.

---

* Den.

Late in the evening I met the young man who had been the first to show me the way to the *kanpa* the day before. He asked me how long I was going to stay, and I answered that I should leave the following day. He also had news to tell me that was rather startling.

The rumour had circulated in the district that a *peelin** had walked about alone in the disguise of a Tibetan and that the *dsongpön*† had sent out several detachments of soldiers to comb the district! If *I* was the person to whom the attention of the *dsongpön* had been drawn, and no other Westerner happened to be travelling in the region, this difficulty may have been the deliberate work of someone in the Underground City. There I had not made the slightest attempt to hide the fact that I was a Westerner. I had not even dyed my face during the three days I had spent in the Valley of Mystery.

Now rapid flight was necessary. Fortunately, about two days' walk at top speed would suffice to enable me to reach the region inhabited by the hermits, where I would, no doubt, receive valuable assistance and protection.

I contemplated leaving immediately, but as I had announced my intention to stay just before I heard the news that a Westerner was being searched for in the district, I could not suddenly alter my decision without giving rise to suspicion.

I felt some concern about the matter, all the more so as I had thrown Narbu's letter away.

I stayed in my den all evening, and late in the

---

* White person.   † District Governor.

morning I went over to the house to attend the lecture, intending to leave immediately after the discussion following the talk given by the Gentle Friend.

That day he lectured on "nothingness", on "becoming like nothing", and the "happiness one derived from becoming like nothing". So there we were! What *motive* did he recommend for seeking a non-egocentrical conception of life? Happiness! The search for happiness!

Not a word about the intense suffering of a man who feels one with all the joys and sorrows of the world. All he recommended was an escape from life, "nothingness", and subsequent happiness, viz. the very height of selfishness.

Before he withdrew I looked at him fully for the last time. There was nothing in his eyes, voice, or bearing that could have provided any clue as to whether he really believed in the destructive things he had said or whether he was a mere tool. He may have been the latter. In most cases, apostles who are themselves deceived are very dangerous. It is easier to deceive people if the deceiver believes in his own message.

I realized how dreadfully clever and adaptable the Evil One is, and in how many different and cleverly disguised ways he carries on his soul-snatching activities.

There is the appeal of wealth and power and the snare of excessive care for the needs of the body. Many people sell their souls to get them. Then there is the appeal of spiritual distinctions and Paradises. The City of the Initiates is a soul-snatching centre of this kind. And for people who cannot be caught by either of the two, there are subtle philosophical systems. Decidedly the devil's shop is a well-stocked one ; he caters for all possible tastes, and his snares are everywhere.

The Gentle Friend had left the room and I listened to the discussion that followed.

"Is not the search for happiness in itself a selfish thing ?" asked one of the hearers. He seemed to have taken up the objection I had mentally raised during the lecture. "Yes," said another one. "It is."

"Then there is a contradiction in all this," again observed the other. "We want to be unselfish, and yet we are selfish in wanting to be unselfish."

The other one hesitated for a while and then remarked : "But I feel that my soul does not want it. *I* want happiness, but my *soul* does not want it."

This remark strikingly illustrated the nature of the type of soul-snatching business carried on on the Mountain of Simplicity, and how man's totalitarian consciousness can be split up by "introspection" and his soul subtly separated.

My determination to do everything in life with my whole being and with intense soul-passion became still greater.

At top speed I left the mountain where the Pied Piper plays the tune of simplicity to catch souls. I marched thirty miles that day, hardly stopping to take food.

When I sat down to take my lunch, which consisted of a handful of uncooked barley-meal and a little water, I pulled out a piece of paper and wrote down the following sketch :

THE CLEVER PHILOSOPHERS

Once upon a time there were clever philosophers. They did not believe in the Creator. "We follow our *own* light," they said. And in all matters they only relied on the light of introspection.

Then they came across the Devil.

"What a monster !" said one of them. "What a comfort to know that nothing is real and everything is a mere reflect of ourselves !"

"You are right," put in a second philosopher. "Everything is subjective ; nothing is objective."

Then the Devil opened his mouth and swallowed them.

When they arrived inside the Devil's body the clever philosophers said with a superior smile :

"Is it not obvious that we were right ? The monster has disappeared."

When I had returned from Asia I found this piece of paper which had passed through the hands of several brigands and the inevitable soaking by rain and occasional spills. The sketch is an accurate picture of the mental condition of the circle of listeners on the Mount of Simplicity. They seem to ignore the polarity of good and evil.

The same afternoon I saw one of the two flying lamas* whom I have described in my earlier book.

Just after sunset I passed a place obviously used for cutting up corpses, which is the usual method of disposing of the dead in Tibet. The relatives hand the body over to the *lag-pas*† and the latter

---

* The flying lamas are called *lun-gom-pas*, which, literally translated, means "air-meditation people" or "wind-meditation people".

† "Hands" or corpse-cutters.

carry them to a place usually marked by white stone slabs where the flesh is cut off and thrown to birds who gather for this strange meal when they see the *lag-pas* approach in the distance. Sometimes the relatives accompany the funeral procession, but in many cases they do not do so, and the corpse-cutters—who are often accompanied by a lama—are left to do their "work" unaccompanied by the relatives of the deceased.

These places used for corpse-cutting are a favourite spot for the sorceries and conjurations of the Tibetan *tantrikas* and *nagpas*.*

As I was in a great hurry I did not want to lose time in going round the place in a wide circle. A few magicians were seated there and performed their strange rites with human bones from corpses whose flesh had been cut off recently. One of the sorcerers beckoned to me to keep far away, but since I had heard on the mountain that the district was being combed to find a white intruder, I was anxious to get to the abodes of the hermits as rapidly as possible, and in spite of his energetic signs I passed the place at a distance of only about fifty yards.

The magicians seemed to resent very greatly that I had disturbed the conjurations for which they had specially chosen the time of the day soon after sunset. They interrupted their sorceries and approached in a threatening attitude, one of them actually swinging a *kha-twam-ya*, a tantric staff with not less than three human skulls fixed at the top! By that time I had met the most sinister forces of Tibet

---

* Black magicians.

and perhaps the whole world, so I did not feel uncomfortable at all when I saw all these magicians approach in a threatening manner. When they were quite near I saw that they were almost furious and looked like so many dogs disturbed while taking their meal. The *tantrikas* almost snarled. They were what a Tibetan would call *hana-honi*.*

I was not afraid of them. I knew that black magicians were not nearly so dreadful as the *grey* ones, viz. those who gave themselves the outer appearance of angels and saviours.

They surrounded me, each of them blowing a strong breath right into my face.

"May the Creator punish you for that," I thought, and remained standing motionless, merely concentrating all my soul-power so as to counteract any possible tendency at 'dissociation' of my personality.

Suddenly one of the black magicians shouted in an agonized voice, *"Chom-den-da!"*† and they all took to their heels. They all ran away in wild terror and disappeared from sight as if a sudden apparition had emerged behind me inspiring them with great fear. One of the "blacks" even left his *kha-twam-ya* behind, since these sticks are rather bulky and prevent fast running.

I could never really find out *why* these *tantrikas* had taken to flight so suddenly. I am not aware of having done anything to inspire them with such terror.

Night had fallen, but I decided to walk on in the

---

* Extremely furious.   † "The conqueror!"

dark, although the countryside was very mountainous, and I fully realized the risk of doing so.
I had to consider the alternative of capture if
these reports about the District Governor having
heard of the presence of a white man were true.
So I had the choice between two dangers of a
different type, and decided to take my chances
on one of both. I should have done better to wait
until daybreak instead of walking on in the dark
night in the mountainous district, which, as I
found a little later, was a very foolish thing to do.

I had not the faintest idea that I still had to pass
through one of the most dreadful ordeals of my
whole Tibetan journey before I reached my goal,
the region inhabited by most of the wise hermits
who stand for the Creator and isolate themselves
in these districts not in order to get selfish bliss,
but in a spirit of sacrifice to counteract in some
measure the dreadful psychical currents set loose
by the various Saviours and the host of fallen
angels incarnated in the flesh in Tibet.

There may be a few such people even in Western
countries, veritable guardian angels of humanity
sometimes incarnated in heroes who counteract
the pernicious working of certain Saviours, but
no spiritual being has a right to tell people who
is a hero and who is the mouthpiece of fallen
angels. Each one must discover this for himself.

I walked on at top speed in the darkness. The
moon had not yet risen, but the starlit sky showed
the way and provided a very dim light enabling me
to avoid the worst precipices. How different had
been the mildly undulating landscape in Northern

Tibet when Ke Shu Kha Ru, the brigand boy, and I had been hunted by the robbers !

As I had no blanket I intended to walk on until sunrise and to sleep then until noon.

Soon after midnight, while I was walking on a gentle slope, it seemed as if the whole ground on which I was moving began to give way in the darkness. A few seconds later I was swept down into the abyss. A portion of my equipment, including the bag containing most of my food, was torn away, while I somersaulted in tremendous bumps down the precipice. Having covered about two hundred yards in this manner, the few seconds seeming to be as long as whole ages, I felt that the ground sloped less and less, and finally I came to a standstill. I was unable to move. Half of my clothes had been torn away while I had somersaulted across debris, and perhaps the eighth part of my skin had been lacerated while I "progressed" in this manner. I thought something had happened to my spine as I was unable to move my trunk. I also felt dreadful pain in my left foot. In this condition I lay on the ground with practically all my food lost and the night getting colder and colder. I knew I was twenty-five miles from the nearest human abode, and now had ample time to meditate on the risks of a solitary explorer who makes the mistake of walking in the mountains by night in uninhabited territories.

For two days and two nights I lay paralysed on the same spot, exposed to the scorching rays of the sun in the afternoon and to the bitter cold by night. I went through all the agonies of cold, thirst, and helplessness of a kind that seemed unendurable. I realized that even courage when it is carried to the point of foolhardiness may be a sin and that it is not enough to avoid sinning against the Creator and against our neighbour, but that man also has obligations towards *himself*. Never before had I felt with such bitter intensity that there was also such a thing as sinning against one's self.

But during those dreadful two days while I lay helpless in the mountains exposed to all kinds of material sufferings and mental agonies, I never blamed the Creator. "Thy will be done," I murmured. I had committed a sin against myself by exposing myself to danger without absolute necessity, and fully realized that I deserved punishment.

As I lay there, forlorn and hopeless, with gushing wounds, I felt that my fate was enviable in comparison with those who had given their souls to the Evil One. In all my self-caused misery I still was a child of the Creator, and in all my agony I never uttered the prayer of "My God, take my sufferings away."

I felt that the laws of the universe were just and that I could not importune the Creator with selfish prayers. I had caused my own dreadful predicament and as a man I had to face the consequences of my blunder. I, the tiny creature, could not ask the Creator to violate the order of His universe and to modify His wise laws of absolutely just retribution in order to please me and take away from me the punishment I had so well deserved.

After all, who was I, and who was the Creator?

When I contemplated His Majesty I felt the distance which separated Him from His creatures. How can the creature fathom God? It would be like a butterfly trying to fathom the greatness of Shakespeare.

The third day I found, with great joy, that I could move a little. The flesh wounds were healing rapidly and in spite of the dreadful thirst, partly due to loss of blood, I began to feel stronger. A little later I found that my foot was on the mend.

The fourth day I was strong enough to crawl. I still felt much pain in my left foot and could not stand upright, but I crawled along as fast as I could, resting most of my weight on my hands. The first hour I had covered two hundred yards. The following hour the speed had increased to two hundred and fifty yards. It was not much in comparison with the twenty-odd miles still separating me from the abodes of the hermits, but it was better than nothing. I blessed the Creator for having spared me the worst (I might have also injured my hands in the accident), and fell asleep in an exhausted condition.

Instead of wasting my strength by continually rubbing my body as I had done the previous nights, when I was unable to move in the bitter cold, I spent the fifth night crawling along at the rate of perhaps six hundred yards an hour. With iron will-power I kept it up practically all night, and then almost collapsed at daybreak. At noon I was on my way again, and in the afternoon I partly regained the use of my legs. The speed at which I now progressed seemed to me enormous. I covered nearly one and a half miles per hour, and in the evening I shouted repeatedly. The sound of my voice loudly echoed back from the mountains. Every five or ten minutes I shouted. In the great quiet of the atmosphere of Tibet sound-waves travel a long way, and I hoped that some of the hermits might hear me.

The following day I advanced at a speed of nearly two miles an hour. Two hermits heard the faint sound of a human voice.

When they found me I had almost reached the limits of human resistance to cold, exposure, thirst, hunger, and fatigue. I had lost blood, too, but I felt that with an iron will I might still have carried on the struggle for another twenty-four hours before I definitely collapsed.

The hermits—who were no "soul-snatchers" this time, but strong and powerful individuals who were intensely personal and yet acted impersonally —took great care of me. They healed my wounds with almost miraculous rapidity, gave me new clothes, and a day later even recovered the sheepskin containing my rubber boat and a few other items of my equipment which had fallen over the precipice.

They immediately put me on a special diet which seemed to be very strange to their patient, since it chiefly consisted of a kind of salad made of various medicinal plants and garlic. Ever since I had left the Underground City a strange cadaveric smell had clung to me. The hermits noticed the smell, which they said may have been due to magical operations by which a portion of the vitalizing principle of my physical body had been drawn away by black sorcerers and then decomposed by magical practices for the purpose of killing me. They said that since their practices had not succeeded in murdering me, my enemies had probably killed themselves in the effort.

In the hands of these marvellous healers I recovered with extraordinary rapidity, and the third day after my arrival in the district I entered the abode of the brother of my friend who had procured me Tibetan clothes before I had entered the country.

"You have gone through dreadful experiences," he said, immediately after having greeted me. "But had we warned you, you might have missed the greatest experience of your life."

So he knew all about it !

"Must everyone discover spiritual values by passing through spiritual ordeals ?" I asked.

"Yes," he replied. "This is inevitable, for man shapes his own destiny. Of course, the nature of the experiences varies in each case."

"I have become intensely soul-conscious now," I said, "and intensely I-conscious."

"I hope you will not turn into an egotist," he observed smilingly.

"No," I said. "An unreasonably high dose of egotism really denotes lack of personality.* Although I am very personal now, I shall always work for the world without any thought of a spiritual reward."

---

* Animals whose whole energies in life are concentrated on the defence of their "I" have no personality at all. Full I-consciousness is not necessarily brutality and selfishness. Man can be intensely personal and yet *act* quite impersonally.

I intensely realized that the more man approaches
full individualization the more he is conscious
of his duties to the Creator, the rising branch of
life, and himself.

The problem of the world is both an individual
and a collective one. Man modifies his environment by his living example, and man in turn is
influenced by his environment. The multitudes
are largely a product of this environment continually influenced and modified by dynamic
personalities. In most cases strong personalities
are the real friends of mankind rather than those
who recommend an absolutely uncompromising
attitude leading to a futile attitude of spiritual and
material suicide. The province of man is *action*.

In this world of matter, which is really the
battleground for a formidable struggle of two
different spiritualities, the few wise men of Tibet
who are great and dynamic personalities *intensely
personal and yet acting impersonally*, represent a kind of
bodyguard of the Creator which holds in check
the other camp of methodically working "annihila-
tors" and "soul-snatchers".

"Can you perform miracles?" I asked two other
wise men who came to see us the following day.

The three "hermits" smiled meaningly.

I could feel their thoughts. They possessed the
power to rule over the forces of Nature, but their
very nature* prevented them from using those

---

* Certain spiritual laws are *inherent* to the very nature of spiritual beings.
Just as a man simply cannot eat stones or a tree live in a place where sunshine never penetrates, spiritual beings cannot do the spiritual things
which are contrary to their spiritual nature.

powers unless it was absolutely necessary in the service of the Creator.

After a slight pause, one of the wise "hermits"* asked me :

"Suppose one of us performed a so-called miracle here before your eyes, would you take this as a proof of a Divine mission ?"

"I have seen men flying," I answered, "and I have seen the most dreadful types of sorcerers make dead bodies walk. . . . I should take no miracle on earth as a proof of the Divine will. The Creator has laid down his own wise laws ruling the universe. It is not He or His servants who break them.

When I mentioned the word "Creator" they all had tears in their eyes. Did they think of the dreadful spectacle of a world in open revolt against its Maker ?

THE END

---

* The reader will have realized that the term "hermit" is a very inade-quate one in describing the few *genuine* Tibetan hermits who are not contemplative but *dynamic* beings. I have chosen the word "hermit" because they isolate themselves voluntarily in a spirit of sacrifice, but apart from this fact the genuine "hermits" have none of the characteristics of devotion, contemplative bliss and meekness which a Westerner is accustomed to associate with the term "hermit".

TIBETAN LADY

Tantric Lama of the Red-Hat sect exorcising Demons

The exaltation of the Tantric Lama reaches its climax;
he falls into a trance

Alexandra David-Neel (left) with her guide, travelled throughout Tibet in the 1920s and 30s. As one of the first woman travellers to visit Tibet she wrote *Magic and Mystery In Tibet* in 1929. In her book, *Intiations and Initiates In Tibet*, David-Neel claims that the man in the lower left (below) is capable of hypnotising and killing at a distance. Such a person person is generally thought to be linked to a black occult fraternity, often the Bon religion of Tibet.

Stone offerings to the Tree Spirits

NEPALI LADY

NEPALI LADY

MALAYSIA
Singapore & Brunei
The Traveller's Guide

by Stefan Loose & Renate Ramb.
This fourth book in the Traveller's
Guide Series is an indispensable
compendium of up-to-date
information for anyone travelling to
these countries, whether its advice
on bamboo huts to local customs.
With the most detailed maps and
travel information of any guide series,
we think these are the best guides in
the world! 460 pages, 5x8 tradepaper.
Hundreds of maps, illustrations and
color photos. $15.95

THAILAND AND BURMA:
The Traveller's Guide

by Doring, Loose, and Ramb. A more
detailed guide on the wonders of
Thailand & Burma, with important
cultural and religious information for
these two Buddhist countries.
Contains an abundance of helpful
advice on accomodation, visas,
transport, restaurants, cultural points
of interest, beaches, islands, jungles
and national parks, plus anything else
of importance. Packed with maps
and color photos. 520 pp, 5x7
tradepaper, $12.95.

TURKEY:
The Traveller's Guide

edited by Michael Muller.
Researched by a team of experienced
travellers, this guide gives you all
the information you need on the
entire Aegean and Mediterranean
coastal areas of Turkey, plus plenty
of information on the interior of one
of the most fascinating and historical
countries in Asia. The book covers
West Anatolia, Cappadocia, Konya,
Ankara, Istanbul, Troy, Ephesus, and
other lost cities. Critical info on
accomodation, restaurants, local
transportation and more. 433pp, 5x7
tradepaper, maps, photos (color & b/
w), $12.95.

SOUTHEAST ASIA:
The Traveller's Guide

by Stefan Loose and Renate Ramb.
For the independent adventure, this
excellent guide covers Indonesia,
Malaysia, Singapore, Burma,
Thailand and Brunei. Packed with
great maps and information on
inexpensive hotels, border crossing
tips, air, sea and land travel, local
transport, restaurants, offshore
islands, temples, ruins, museums and
national parks. In addition, there is
good background information on the
respective cultures, on how and how
not to behave, and most importantly,
how to make the best of your trip.
540pp, 5x7 tradepaper, hundreds of
maps & photos (color & b/w). $15.95.

STONEHENGE ...
A closer look
By Bonnie Gaunt

In all the ages since its construction men have built nothing comparable to Stonehenge. Like the Great Pyramid of Gizeh, the solutions to the mystery that surrounds its construction, its architect and its purpose have been sincerely sought by scientists, theologians, archaeologists and historians. Now Stonehenge begins to give up her secrets. The story that it tells not only takes us through 4,000 years of mans history, but far beyond, into the timeless forces of the universe, and into the future of man on this planet. The story of Stonehenge touches the lives of every one of us.

$9.95   ISBN 0-9602688-0-4
236 Pages 47 Line Drawings
5 Black & white photographs
5 x 8 Tradepaper   **NEW RELEASE**

STONEHENGE...
a closer look

BONNIE GAUNT

PYRAMID ENERGY: THE PHILOSOPHY OF GOD, THE SCIENCE OF MAN
by D & M Hardy and M & K Killick

This book is far more than the title proclaims. It is an exhaustive study of the many energy fields around us, including the purpose of ley lines, megaliths and pyramids, vortex energy, Nikola Tesla's coil energy, tachion energy, levitation, the meaning of the Ark of the Covenant, & more.

$12.95   ISBN 0-9322298-58-7
266 pp 100's of Photos & Diagrams
6 x 9 Tradepaper

THE MAGNIFICENT NUMBERS OF THE GREAT PYRAMID AND STONEHENGE
By Bonnie Gaunt

On the rocky plateau of Gizeh, fifteen miles from Cairo, stands the world's most amazing wonder, the Great Pyramid. It stands silent and serene against the Egyptian sky, yet its very presence is a bold defiance against time, a sacred memorial to the intelligence of its builders and their knowledge of time, space, and the universe. Each new generation of man has marveled at this magnificent monument. This ancient wonder has become a modern mystery. The amazing corelation of its geometry with ancient Stonehenge, the earth, sun, and moon gives us insight into its purpose and its builder. The story that it tells touches us with wonder, and fills us with a profound respect for its architect.

$9.95 ISBN 0-9602688-1-2
216 pp   97 Line drawings
23 Black & white photographs
5 x 8 Tradepaper
   NEW RELEASE

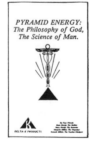

PYRAMID ENERGY:
The Philosophy of God,
The Science of Man.

DELTA-K PRODUCTS

IN SECRET TIBET
Theodore Illion

A reprint of a rare '30s travel book by Illion, an exceptionally resourceful English-German traveler who not only spoke Tibetan, but actually travelled as a Tibetan in a land forbidden to Westerners at the time. His incredible adventures make this one of the most exciting travel books ever published.

210 pp, illustrated, 6 × 9, $15.95, NEW

DARKNESS OVER TIBET
Theodore Illion

In this second volume of travel adventures, the author journeys through the remotest regions of Tibet, is invited to a secret underground city, and barely escapes to tell his tale.

210 pp, illustrated, 6 × 9, $15.95, NEW

VIMANA AIRCRAFT OF ANCIENT INDIA & ATLANTIS

by David Hatcher Childress.
Introduction by
Dr. Ivan T. Sanderson.

This may be the most controversial science book ever written! To the established scientific community the idea that ancient Indians flew around in airships of a technology equivalent to our own would be too fantastic to discuss. This thick and well illustrated volume is a virtual compendium on the fascinating subject of "Vimana" aircraft, a type of airship allegedly developed more than 10,000 years ago in the ancient Rama Empire of India and the "Atlantis". Contains just about every reference ever made to vimanas and "vailixi" (as the Atlantean versions of these aircraft were supposedly called) in ancient and recent literature. Diagrams and photos of airships, plus the entire 4th Century B.C. text on Vimanas, the *Vimanika Shastra* text translated by Dr. Josyer of the University of Mysore. 320 pp, 8x10 tradepaper, photos, diagrams & illustrations. $15.95 January Publication.

ASIAN VOYAGES
TO AMERICA
500 B.C.

NU SUN

NEW!

NU SUN:
Asian American Voyages 500 BC
by Gunnar Thompson.
This large and attractive book tells the true story of ancient Chinese voyages to North America and the amazing account of their colonial settlements. Incredible revelations about the mysterious origins of the Mayans and the Taoist source of Chinese & Mayan religious symbolism. More than 500 illustrations of actual artifacts. 240 pp, 8x11 Hardback. Profusely illustrated, with bibliography & index. $23.95

ANTI-GRAVITY &
THE UNIFIED FIELD

edited by David Hatcher Childress.
Is Einstein's Unified Field the answer to all of our energy problems? Explored are the controversial subjects of how magnetism, electricity and gravity manifest from a Unified Field around us, UFO propulsion, gravity control, vortex technology, suppressed inventions, Nikola Teslas anti-gravity airships, anti-mass generators, gravity waves and free energy are all dealt with in depth. A bit of humour is added in the end with the comics section. 307 pp 100's of Photo's & Drawings, 7 X 10 Tradepaper. **$14.95**

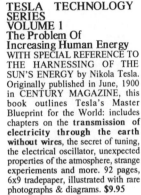

TESLA TECHNOLOGY SERIES
VOLUME 1
The Problem Of
Increasing Human Energy

WITH SPECIAL REFERENCE TO THE HARNESSING OF THE SUN'S ENERGY by Nikola Tesla. Originally published in June, 1900 in CENTURY MAGAZINE, this book outlines Tesla's Master Blueprint for the World: includes chapters on the **transmission of electricity through the earth without wires**, the secret of tuning, the electrical oscillator, unexpected properties of the atmosphere, strange experiments and more. 92 pages, 6x9 tradepaper, illustrated with rare photographs & diagrams. **$9.95**

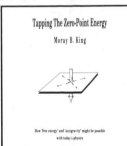

THE ANTI-GRAVITY HANDBOOK

edited by D. H. Childress.
Now into several printings, this fascinating compilation of material, some of it humorous, explores the theme of gravity control and the theoretical propulsion technique used by UFOs. Chapters include "How To Build a Flying Saucer", Quartz Crystals and Anti-Gravity, Arthur C. Clarke on Gravity Control, NASA, the Moon and Anti-Gravity, & flying saucer patents. There is also a rare article by Nikola Tesla entitled "A Machine to End All War".
$12.95. 195 pp.
100's of Photos Drawings & Patents 7x10 tradepaper.

TAPPING THE ZERO POINT ENERGY

by Moray B. King.
The author, a well-known researcher, explains how "free energy" and "anti-gravity" might be possible with todays physics. The theories of the zero point energy show there are tremendous fluctuations of electrical field energy imbedded within the fabric of space and how in the 1930s the inventor T. Henry Moray could produce a fifty kilowatt "free energy" machine; how the Pons / Fleischmann "Cold Fusion" experiment could produce tremendous heat without fusion; how certain experiments might produce a gravitational anomaly. 6x9 tradepaper, 170pp, illustrations, diagrams, bibliography, **$9.95.**

ANTI-GRAVITY AND THE WORLD GRID

edited by D.H. Childress.
Is the earth surrounded by an intricate electromagnetic grid network offering free energy? This complex pattern of the earth's energies, researchers believe, if properly understood, can shed light on the nature of gravity, UFO's, vortex areas, power spots, ley lines, and even the placement of ancient megalithic structures. One of our best selling books—fascinating and visual, 267 pp 100's of Photos & Drawings
7x10 tradepaper. **$12.95.**

Ordering Instructions

Mail in the Order Form. Please Print all information. Please do not send cash.
Remit the amount due by check or money order.
When paying by Credit Card be sure to include your signature and telephone #.
We accept telephone credit card orders. Call anytime **815 253 6390**
We give a **10 % discount** when you **order 3 or more items.**
BACKORDERS:
We will backorder forthcoming and out-of stock titles unless otherwise requested.
RETAILERS:
Standard discounts available
Call or write for more information
SHIPPING CHARGES: United States
Postal Bookrate :
$1.50 for 1st book
50¢ each additional book.
United Parcel Service (UPS):
$3.00 for 1st Book
50¢ each additional item.
(street addresses only)
Airmail:
$5.00 per item
Sorry , No C.O.D.
Residents of Illinois
add 7% sales tax.
SHIPPING CHARGES: Canada
Postal Bookrate :
$2.00 for 1st book
50¢ each additional book.
Airmail:
$6.00 per item
SPECIAL PAYMENT NOTICE
FOR CANADIAN ORDERS
1. Remittance **MUST BE** $US.
2. Canadian Postal Money Orders Accepted.
3. No Personal checks.
4. Other Checks **MUST BE** drawn on a US Bank.
Shipping Charges: All other Countries
Surface Delivery:
$4.00 1st item.
$1.00 each addition item.
Airmail: $10.00 per book.
SPECIAL PAYMENT NOTICE
FOR INTERNATIONAL ORDERS
1. Remittance **MUST BE** $US
2. Checks MUST BE drawn on an American Bank.
3. Add $5.00 for airmail subscription to future catalogs

☐ Check here if this is a new address

Name_____

Address _____

City_____ State_____ Postal Code_____

Telephone (home)_____(work)_____

Catalog Item Description	Price	Qty	$ Amount

Adventures Unlimited Press
Post Office Box 22
Stelle, Illinois 60919-9899
815 - 253 - 6390

Item Totals	
Less Discount	
Sales Tax	
Shipping	
Total Remit	

☐ Check enclosed
☐ Please charge this to my **Mastercard/ VISA**   [MasterCard] [VISA]
Card Number_____
Exp. Date_____ Signature_____

Send a catalog to a Friend

Name_____
Address_____
City_____State_____ZIP_____

Box 22 Stelle, Il 60919   815